LIVERPOOL
THE CITY AT A GLANCE

Museum of Liverpool
The Pier Head buildings (see p026) are known as Liverpool's Three Graces, but do the modern structures on Mann Island constitute its disgraces? Some complain that the zigzag profiles jar with the adjacent slice of history.
See p014

West Tower
This mainly residential tower by architects Aedas became the city's tallest in 2007. The Panoramic 34 restaurant (see p038) sits atop.
Brook Street

Stanley Dock Tobacco Warehouse
With 14 storeys and 14.5 hectares of storage space, Anthony Lyster's 1901 depot was said to be the largest brick building in the world.
Great Howard Street

St John's Beacon
There's little love for this 138m futurist spire, built in 1969 as a ventilation shaft. It is now the HQ of Radio City; take a tour for the views.
1 Houghton Street, T 472 6800

St George's Hall
Arguably the UK's finest neoclassical pile was designed by Harvey Lonsdale Elmes.
St George's Place, T 225 6911

Adelphi Hotel
Once the most splendid hotel outside London, R Frank Atkinson's Adelphi opened in 1914, its interiors echoing the cruise ships whose passengers it hosted. Its glories are long gone.
Ranelagh Place, T 709 7200

St Luke's Church
Events from gigs to screenings are held in the roofless interior of the 'bombed-out church'.
Berry Street, T 709 7562

INTRODUCTION
THE CHANGING FACE OF THE URBAN SCENE

Liverpool's great port opened the door to 200 years of prosperity and fostered a sense of otherness that endures to this day. Steeped in maritime wanderlust, this proud city has long identified more with the US than home shores. Always alert to the next vagary in its fortunes – a legacy of dock-labour casualism – the locals' wariness is entirely justified right now. Regeneration has tweaked the urban landscape ever since the 1980s, yet if the totemic 40-year Liverpool Waters proposal goes ahead in anything like its original guise, the London Docklands-style transformation of 60 hectares of mainly derelict (yet historically significant) riverfront will redefine the city.

Whatever happens to the northern docks, one of Liverpool's strongest draws remains its architecture: displays of its historical might as a global commercial hub, from trade institutions to great brick warehouses and immaculate Georgian terraces. After the late 20th-century crash, many a handsome building found itself lacking occupier or purpose. Developers exploited the faded grandeur of these shells, producing a roster of lively bars and restaurants that chime with the Scouse passion for dressing up and hitting town. Yet Liverpool does highbrow too. It has the greatest collection of galleries, museums and listed buildings outside the capital – not to mention an unrivalled musical heritage. As European Capital of Culture in 2008, it redoubled its creative energy, which continues its full expression in the increasingly vibrant Biennial art festival.

ESSENTIAL INFO
FACTS, FIGURES AND USEFUL ADDRESSES

TOURIST OFFICE
Anchor Courtyard
Albert Dock
T 233 2008
www.visitliverpool.com

TRANSPORT
Car hire
Enterprise
T 709 4999
Ferries
Mersey Ferries
T 330 1000
www.merseyferries.co.uk
Taxis
T 922 7373
www.deltataxis.net
There are cab ranks in the city centre
Trains
Merseyrail
www.merseyrail.org
Trains run from approximately 6am to just before midnight

EMERGENCY SERVICES
Ambulance
T 999
Late-night pharmacy
(until 11pm; 9.30pm at weekends)
Lloyds
Unit C2
Prospect Point
Prescot Street
T 264 0178
www.lloydspharmacy.com

EMBASSIES
US Embassy
24 Grosvenor Square
London
T 020 7499 9000
london.usembassy.gov

POSTAL SERVICES
Post office
WHSmith Liverpool ONE
1-3 South John Street
T 707 6606
Shipping
DHL
Riverside House
Estuary Boulevard
Speke
T 0844 248 0844

BOOKS
Liverpool: Shaping the City
by Stephen Bayley (RIBA)
The Mersey Sound by Roger McGough, Brian Patten and Adrian Henri (Penguin)

WEBSITES
Architecture
www.liverpoolarchitecture.com
Art/Culture
www.thedoublenegative.co.uk
Newspaper
www.liverpooldailypost.co.uk

EVENTS
Biennial
www.biennial.com

COST OF LIVING
Taxi from Manchester Airport to Liverpool city centre
£50
Cappuccino
£2.40
Packet of cigarettes
£8
Daily newspaper
£0.55
Bottle of champagne
£50

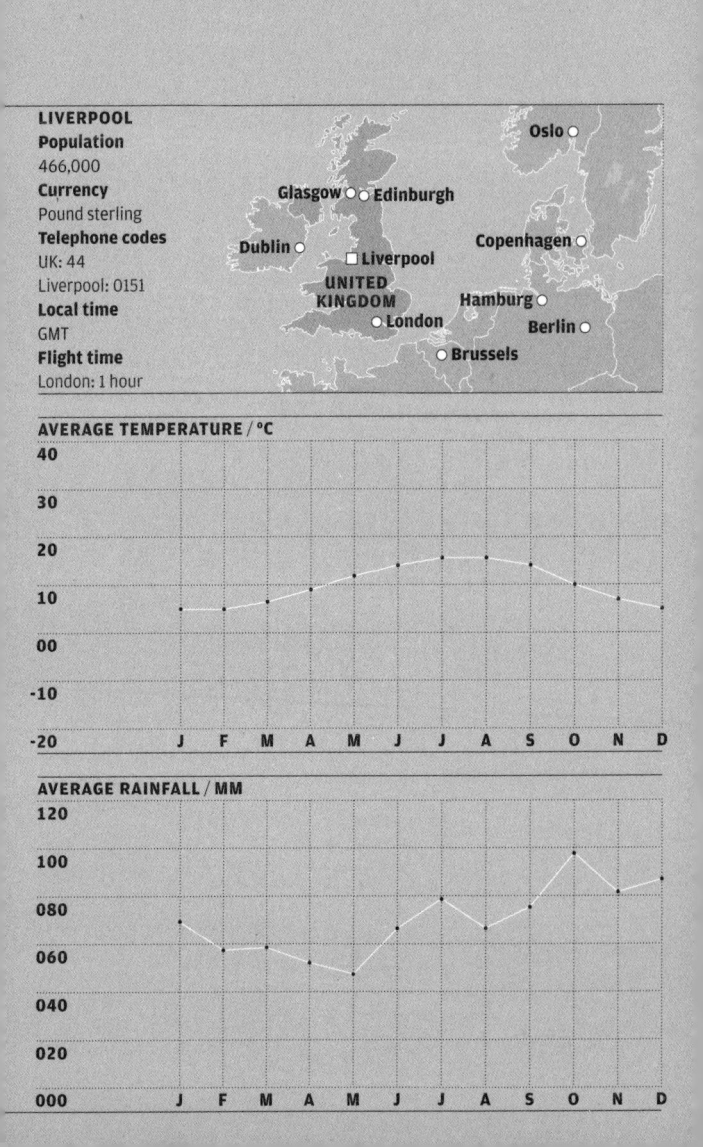

LIVERPOOL
Population
466,000
Currency
Pound sterling
Telephone codes
UK: 44
Liverpool: 0151
Local time
GMT
Flight time
London: 1 hour

AVERAGE TEMPERATURE / °C

AVERAGE RAINFALL / MM

NEIGHBOURHOODS
THE AREAS YOU NEED TO KNOW AND WHY

To help you navigate the city, we've chosen the most interesting districts (see below and the map inside the back cover) and colour-coded our featured venues, according to their location; those venues that are outside these areas are not coloured.

BALTIC TRIANGLE
By day this is a place of small industry; by night it was largely deserted until Camp and Furnace (see p028) flung open its doors. Further draws are Elevator Studios and its café bar (25-31 Parliament Street, T 707 1137), the Gustaf Adolf Nordic church (138 Park Lane) and the nearby Cains Brewery (Stanhope Street, T 709 8734).

LIME ST/WILLIAM BROWN ST
Glenn Howells Architects' £9m refurb of Lime Street Station restored the Victorian building's looks and decluttered this city portal. Now, you step out to a view of the magnificent St George's Hall (St George's Place, T 225 6911) and Walker Art Gallery (William Brown Street, T 478 4199).

CENTRAL DOCKS
Despite the scrubbing up of Albert Dock in the 1980s and the contemporary Mann Island development, there's something timeless about the work of 19th-century dock engineer Jesse Hartley and his successors. The Three Graces (see p026) form the very heart of Liverpool.

ROPEWALKS/CHINATOWN
Europe's highest Chinese arch isn't as much of a draw as all the independent boutiques and nightlife ventures in this part of town. This is where developer Urban Splash made its name – projects include the Tea Factory (82 Wood Street), Vanilla Factory (39 Fleet Street) and St Peter's Church (see p060).

UNIVERSITY/GEORGIAN QUARTER
Two cathedrals and two universities are just the start of the pickings here. There are fine Georgian terraces on Rodney and Canning Streets, and Falkner Square is all faded 1840s grandeur. There's culture, too, in the Everyman Theatre (Hope Street, T 709 4776), under redevelopment till late 2013, and Philharmonic Hall (see p036).

MOORFIELDS
This is the city's most disparate patch. Beatles fans cluster on Mathew Street; gay venues dot Stanley, Cumberland, Eberle and Temple Streets; and the business district is centred on Old Hall Street: check out St Paul's Square, the Cotton Exchange and Oriel Chambers (see p074).

COMMERCIAL DISTRICT
Church Street was for a long time the city's principal retail stretch but the centre of gravity has now been skewed south by Liverpool ONE (see p078), a £1bn shopping-led complex that extends over 17 hectares and links to Albert Dock via Pelli Clarke Pelli and BDP's landscaped Chavasse Park.

BIRKENHEAD
For many Liverpudlians, the Wirral is a hazily defined expanse 'over the water', yet it's only 1,125m across the Mersey from the Pier Head. The splendour of Hamilton Square and Birkenhead Park is evidence of the wealth of the well-to-do merchants who set up home here in the 19th century.

LANDMARKS
THE SHAPE OF THE CITY SKYLINE

As a maritime city, it's not surprising that Liverpool's most famous bevy of architectural beauties – the Three Graces – are sited at the Pier Head (see p026). Yet an inland cluster outshines them. Harvey Lonsdale Elmes' St George's Hall (St George's Place, T 225 6911), from 1854, is perhaps the UK's finest expression of neoclassicism, and William Brown Street is a parade of Victorian splendour that includes the grandiose 1877 Walker Art Gallery (T 478 4199).

Liverpool generally does functional bulk better than statement height, prime examples being the 1902 red-brick Cains Brewery (Stanhope Street, T 709 8734), the Littlewoods Building (overleaf) and the 1957 Tate & Lyle Silo (Regent Road, Huskisson Dock). And although the centre has seen a proliferation of high-rises since Ian Simpson's 2004 Beetham Tower (110 Old Hall Street), the most successful of which is Unity (see p065), it's all rather piecemeal.

More fondly regarded are the historical and cultural hubs that are firmly woven into the city's fabric and collective consciousness, notably the ruins of St Luke's Church (Berry Street), the Everyman Theatre (13 Hope Street, T 709 4776), Philharmonic pub (see p049) and the 'streaky bacon building', Albion House (James Street), the former White Star Line (and Titanic) HQ. Of course, the docks are Liverpool's raison d'être, and a stroll along the Mersey in either direction from Albert Dock throws up some startling sights.

For full addresses, see Resources.

Littlewoods Building

Liverpool and Littlewoods are inseparable. Founder John Moores' 1920s football pools enterprise came first, followed by a mail-order operation that saw him hailed as 'the housewives' saviour'. It was worth £4m come 1936, only four years after its establishment. The Littlewoods Building was architecture as advert – the 1938 art deco giant is located on the city's eastern approach road overlooking Wavertree Park, its symmetrical white concrete bulk and high clock tower commanding this part of town. The design has been attributed to Gerald de Courcy Fraser, also responsible for iconic department store Lewis's. The behemoth has lain empty in a poor state of repair since 2002, but could get a new lease of life as a hotel and office complex if the council gives the go-ahead.
Edge Lane, near Wavertree Botanic Gardens

011

LANDMARKS

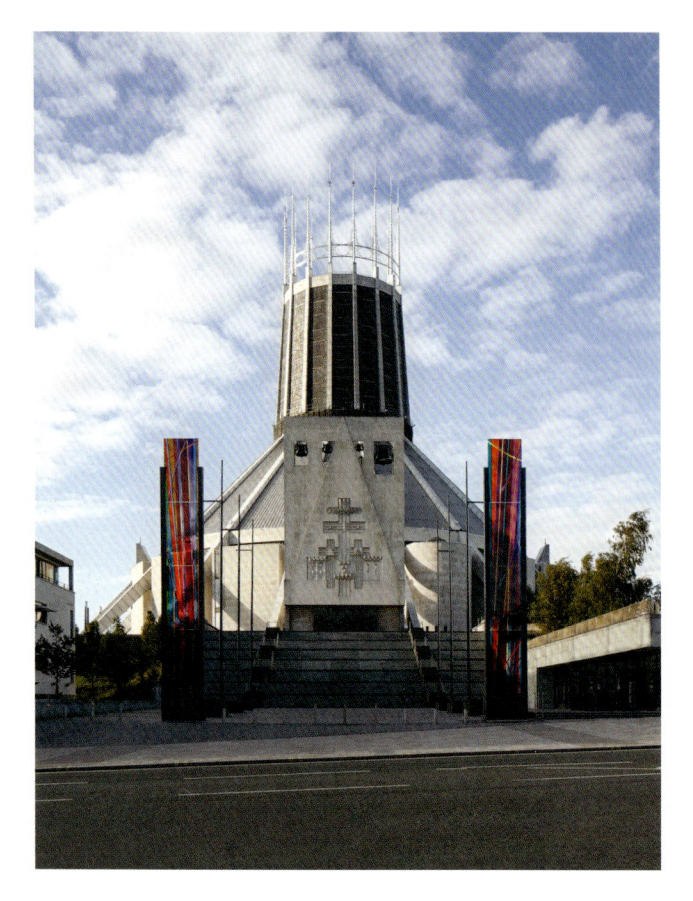

Metropolitan Cathedral
This is the church that Liverpool's Catholics had to make do with after Edwin Lutyens' dream of a building to outstrip St Peter's in Rome was scuppered by WWII and rising costs. Frederick Gibberd's 1967 surrogate was derided by some – 'Paddy's Wigwam' and 'Mersey Funnel' were two jibes – but has stood the test of time. The altar stands at the centre of the circular space (60m in diameter), surrounded by 13 chapels and beautifully lit by John Piper and Patrick Reyntiens' stained glass; a spindly crown evokes thorns. In contrast to the nearby Anglican Cathedral (see p034), which hunkers down heavily, the Met appears ready for lift-off. Take a tour of Lutyens' remarkable crypt – the only part of his design that was completed, in 1958.
Mount Pleasant, T 709 9222,
www.liverpoolmetrocathedral.org.uk

Runcorn Bridge

You have to travel as far as Widnes, 21km south-east of the city centre, to find a bridge that crosses the Mersey. There had been talk of a Liverpool to Birkenhead span since the mid-18th century but tunnel proponents won the day, and the 1934 Queensway Tunnel was the world's longest underwater project of its kind. This Widnes to Runcorn crossing will likely signal your arrival in Liverpool, especially if you're travelling by train. It comprises William Baker's 1868 railway bridge and a 1961 steel through-arch road bridge by Mott, Hay and Anderson (which was widened and renamed 'Silver Jubilee' in 1977) with a cantilevered footpath. To cope with traffic, plans for a six-lane cable-stayed bridge to the east, christened the Mersey Gateway, were approved in 2010.
Runcorn/Widnes

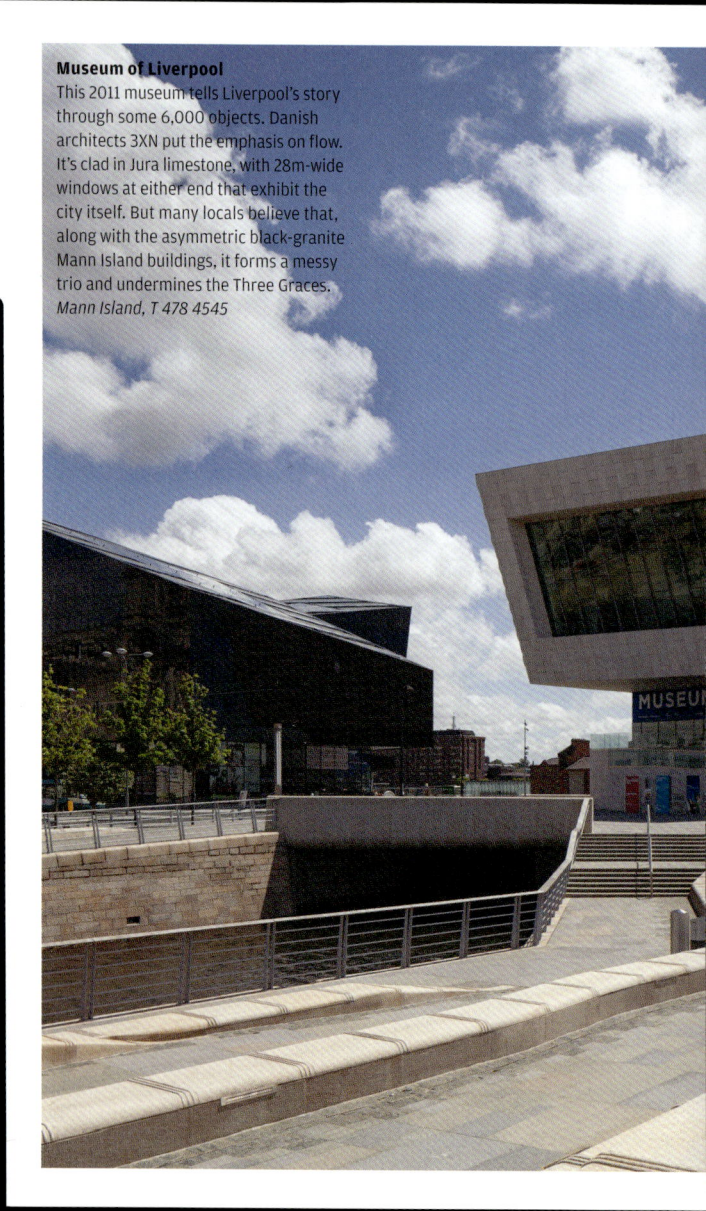

Museum of Liverpool
This 2011 museum tells Liverpool's story through some 6,000 objects. Danish architects 3XN put the emphasis on flow. It's clad in Jura limestone, with 28m-wide windows at either end that exhibit the city itself. But many locals believe that, along with the asymmetric black-granite Mann Island buildings, it forms a messy trio and undermines the Three Graces.
Mann Island, T 478 4545

LANDMARKS

HOTELS

WHERE TO STAY AND WHICH ROOMS TO BOOK

Liverpool regenerated furiously around its 2008 European Capital of Culture award, but hotel investors brought little to the party. However, with the ACC convention centre drawing rising numbers and the reintroduction of turnaround cruises in 2012, there is now greater impetus. Indeed, architects Falconer Chester Hall are busy on three historic projects: turning the 1865 Municipal Annex Building, with its 50 stained-glass windows, into a DoubleTree by Hilton (6 Sir Thomas Street, T 0870 590 9090); converting the 1882 Union House (Victoria Street); and a makeover of the 1903 Royal Insurance Building (1-9 North John Street), with its gilded dome.

Reliable if uninspiring chains include the Radisson Blu (107 Old Hall Street, T 966 1500), Malmaison (7 William Jessop Way, T 229 5000) and Hilton (3 Thomas Steers Way, T 708 4200), which overlooks Albert Dock and attracts a blinged-to-the-nines crowd to its Playground nightclub. There are a few quirky independents, such as The Racquet Club (5 Chapel Street, T 236 6676), which has two squash courts in Sir James Picton's 1859 Hargreaves Building, and Heywood House (11 Fenwick Street, T 224 1444), set in a former bank that dates from 1799, but our choice of stay has long been the Hope Street Hotel (see p018). Over on the Wirral, history buffs can now stay in one of the mews cottages in the grounds of Lord Leverhulme's Thornton Manor (Thornton House, T 353 1155). *For full addresses and room rates, see Resources.*

Leverhulme Hotel
Opened in 1907 as a cottage hospital for Port Sunlight workers, the Leverhulme was converted into a hotel a century later. The mosaic floor in the lobby remains, complemented by art deco touches, walnut doors from a defunct bank and some rather intense carpets. The 19 rooms are spread across a site that includes a new Coach House. Room 108 (above) is the only one of the three Opus Grand Suites in the original building, and has a lovely bay window; Room 109 features a rooftop jacuzzi. In the restaurant, chef Richard Fox's bold flavours draw a loyal crowd. Nearby sister hotel Hillbark (T 625 2400) is a half-timbered Victorian property with stained-glass windows by William Morris, and is a popular wedding venue.
Port Sunlight Village, T 644 6655,
www.leverhulmehotel.co.uk

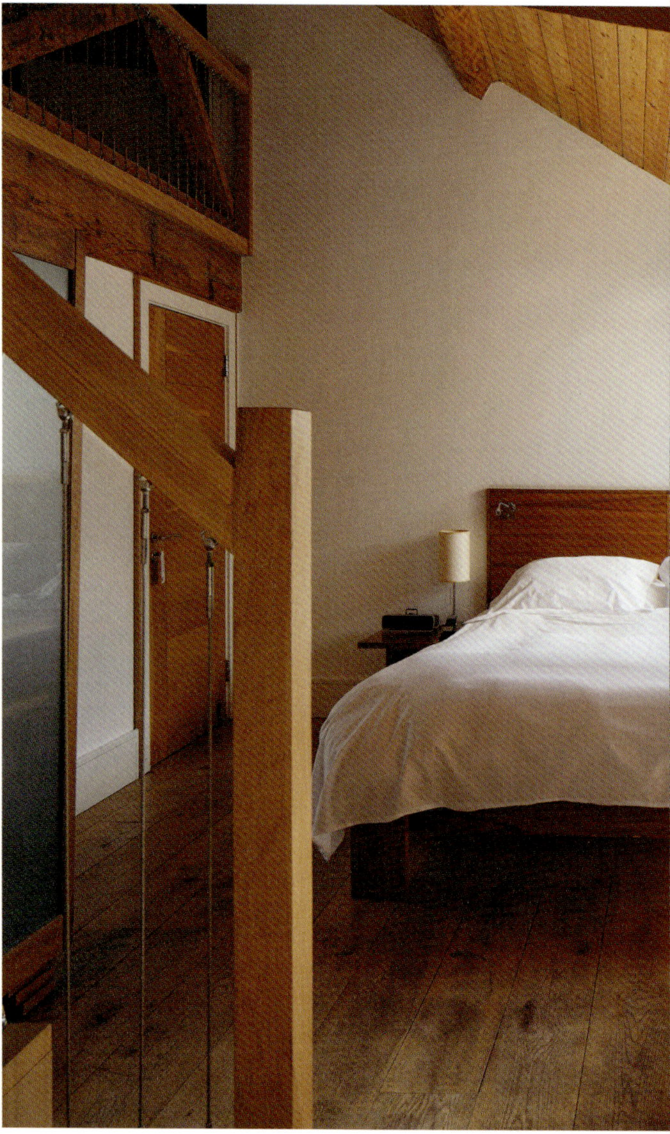

HOTELS

Hope Street Hotel
The understated chic of Liverpool's best boutique hotel has been fashioned out of an 1860s carriage works, built in the style of a Venetian palazzo, and a 1970s police station. It's a riot of texture, all brick, limestone, glass and wood. Of the 89 rooms, No 406 (pictured) has huge pine beams and a mezzanine tub. There is also a fine restaurant (see p040).
40 Hope Street, T 709 3000

Hard Days Night Hotel

Liverpool's heritage is greater than the sum of John, Paul, George and Ringo, but still it was fitting that this Beatles-themed hotel should open in the city's year as European Capital of Culture. Design LSM has incorporated the owners' hoard of memorabilia – Klaus Voormann's album artwork, photos by Bill Zygmant and Paul Saltzman – into a museum-like experience without going OTT. The restaurant, which offers good modern British cooking, is named after *Sgt Pepper* sleeve-designer Peter Blake, and the stylish Bar Four is lined with mahogany and features Moooi 'Smoke' chairs. The McCartney Suite (above) has a tongue-in-cheek ambience that is preferable to the Lennon Suite's startling mock-up of the *Imagine* video.
41-44 North John Street, T 236 1964, www.harddaysnighthotel.com

Albany Apartments

JK Colling's brick and sandstone Albany Building started life in 1858 as a cotton exchange and boasts carvings of stylised foliage on its exterior. It was converted into flats in the noughties and there are a few apartments available to rent, offering the chance to experience this architectural icon at first hand. Cotton was inspected in the iron-bridged courtyard (above), which has been given a makeover by design studio BCA to turn it into the 'Garden of Light', incorporating bespoke trellises, spiralled benches and chandeliers. The decor of the flats themselves is nothing special; bigger draws are the location and the no-groups policy (the city has become a magnet for stag and hen parties).
Old Hall Street, T 0800 699 0490 (one bedroom); T 07778 309 671 (two bedroom), www.come2liverpool.com

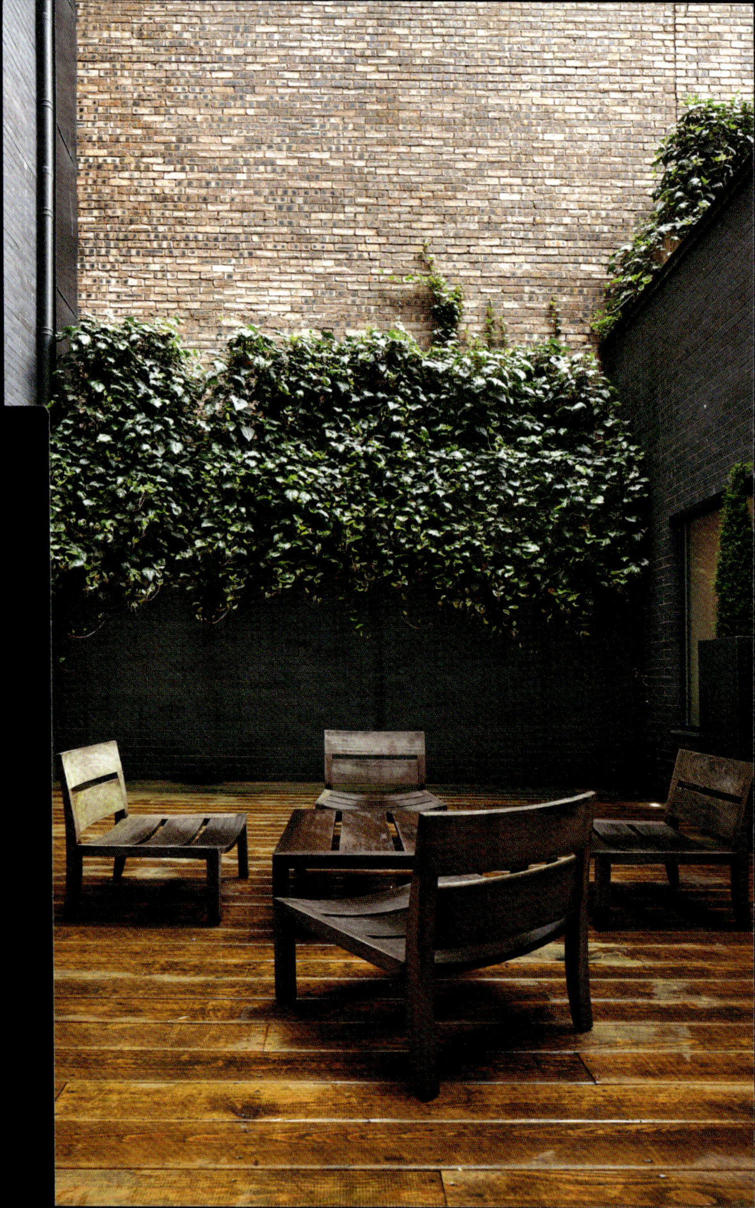

Base2Stay

Architects Austin-Smith:Lord's exemplary reworking of this 19th-century warehouse, formerly an iron foundry and printing press, prettified its brute physicality. It opened as Base2Stay in 2010 and is the city's best no-frills venue – no restaurant or bar, just a cleanly executed space in which to bed down. Lively artworks by Ronald Diennet add interest and the rooms are lent character by the wooden roof trusses that were salvaged from 17th- and 18th-century ships. This is a party street, so you'll be glad of the triple-glazed windows, but planning regulations dictate that they can't be opened. The patio (opposite) of the Secret Garden Suite (above) only gets sun in the morning but it is good for fresh air and seagull cries.
29 Seel Street, T 705 2626,
www.base2stay.com/liverpool/the-hotel

24 HOURS
SEE THE BEST OF THE CITY IN JUST ONE DAY

Liverpool is defined by the river, so after breakfast in Birkenhead, begin your day with the boat ride immortalised by Gerry and the Pacemakers. The ferry across the Mersey gives unrivalled views of the post-industrial landscape and waterfront architecture that owes much to early 20th-century US trends, although more recent arrivals like the Museum of Liverpool (see p014) and Broadway Malyan's oft-criticised Mann Island have skewed the appearance of this iconic stretch. To see the whole city laid out before you, the best perspectives to be had are from the Anglican Cathedral (see p034) and the 91m-high Panoramic 34 restaurant (see p038).

After a glance at Open Eye (see p027) – just one gallery in a city collection that is arguably the most impressive in the UK outside the capital – it's a 15-minute stroll for lunch at Camp and Furnace (see p028) in the Baltic Triangle; still rough around the edges, but all the more fascinating for it. FACT (see p030) is a progressive mix of new media and arthouse; The Bluecoat (see p032) and the Philharmonic (see p036) are institutions that have been around rather longer. However, since seamen came ashore clutching US rock'n'roll 45s in the 1950s, popular music has remained the city's cultural preoccupation. Avoid the naff Beatles mecca of Mathew Street and look for promoters like Deep Hedonia, Evol, Harvest Sun and Samizdat; or anything hosted by The Kazimier (see p052). *For full addresses, see Resources.*

10.00 Home

Mersey Ferries' River Explorer Cruise stops at Seacombe and progresses to Woodside, where you should disembark for breakfast at Home. This light-touch 2009 conversion of the 1864 ferry terminal booking hall has Tom Dixon lighting above the bar, oversized pendants and Konstantin Grcic furniture. Bag a table on the mezzanine, which was constructed from former landing-stage buildings, for some widescreen river views. You'll be overlooking the scene of much transatlantic emigration, so it's appropriate that breakfast options at this delightful spot range from Welsh rarebit to brioche French toast and US-style pancakes. Home has a sister café in Oxton (T 653 7552), close to Fraiche (see p056), where you can perch on Eames and Robin Day chairs.
Woodside Ferry Approach, T 330 1475, www.homecoffee.co.uk

11.00 Pier Head

When George's Dock was infilled at the turn of the 20th century it recalibrated the waterfront, and the trio of US-influenced buildings at the Pier Head symbolises the city's shifting self-image from port-made-good to global gateway. The Port of Liverpool Building was completed in 1907, with its cherry-on-the-cake dome added at the last minute. For statement-making, though, it's no match for the Royal Liver Building (above; 1908-11), where architect Walter Aubrey Thomas worked François Hennebique's ferro-concrete technique into Europe's first high-rise. The iconic Liver Birds perch on top, designed by German Carl Bartels. The middle of the 'Three Graces' came last (above, right; 1916-1917), built for the Cunard Shipping Line. Ask the concierge if you can take a look inside its ornate, cavernous lobby.

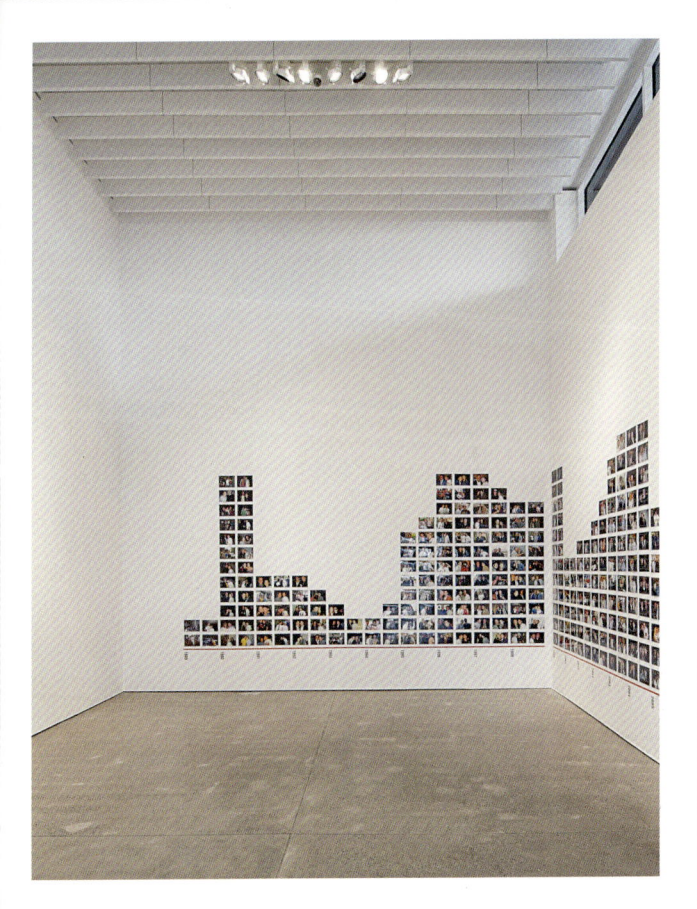

11.30 Open Eye Gallery
This was one of the UK's first photography galleries, founded in 1977. Martin Parr's 'The Last Resort' started life as a 1985 exhibition here, and the archive includes treasures by Edward Chambré Hardman, whose perfectly preserved 1950s Rodney Street house and studio (T 709 6261) is well worth a visit. Open Eye moved premises regularly, an itinerant tendency that matches its rich documentary heritage, and found a home in 2011 on Mann Island. The main space hosts major contemporary shows: Mitch Epstein's 'American Power' launched the site, and Richard Simpkins' self-study into celebrity culture, 'Richard & Famous' (above), was a hit. An exterior wall clad in translucent Corian designed by architects RCKa is used for art installations.
19 Mann Island, T 236 6768, www.openeye.org.uk

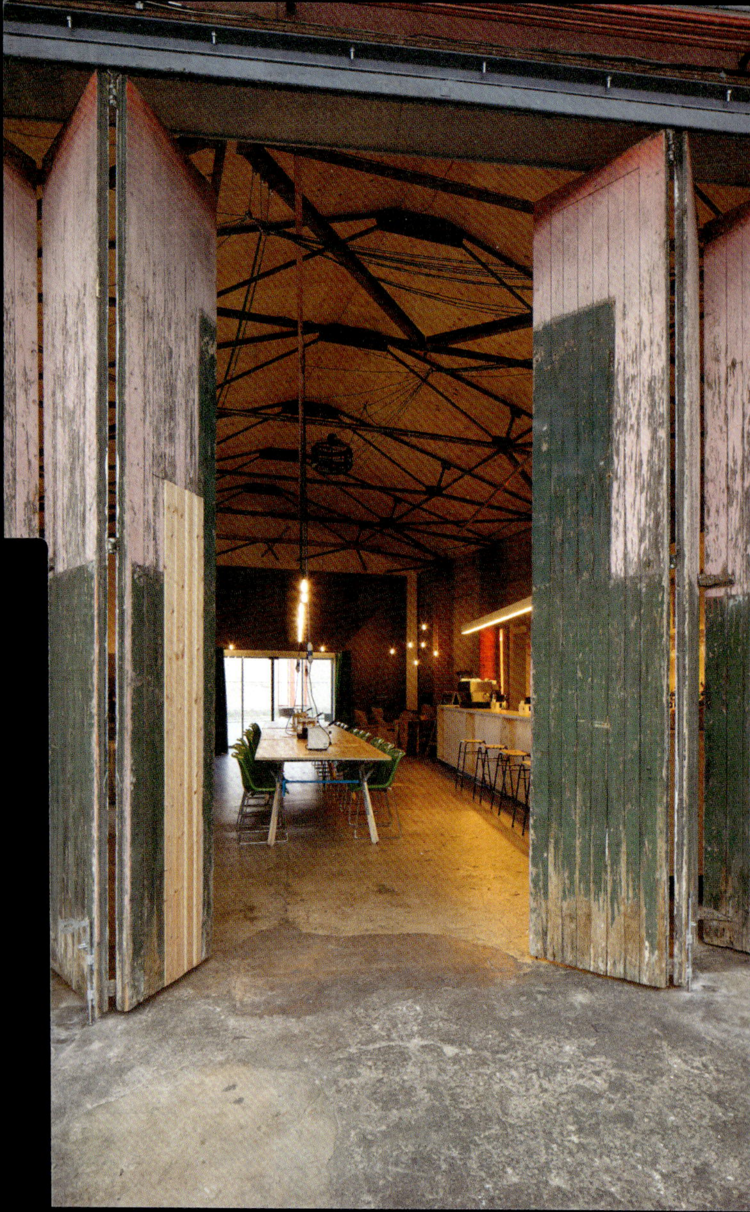

13.00 Camp and Furnace

The name Furnace is appropriate, as this venue is the Baltic Triangle's engine room, attracting new traffic to the gentrifying area. Architects FVMA and design agency Smiling Wolf have made a virtue of the raw industrial feel. Installed in the 'lobby' (opposite) are a DIY plywood bar, an open fire and a communal table, above which dangle bulbs and sockets. Here, chef Steven Burgess' food is Liverpool's finest at this price; we suggest sharing a Poacher or Shepherd platter. Alternatively, dine in the eponymous furnace room (above), where Sunday roasts are served. A number of vintage caravans are parked (the 'camp' part) in a larger space used for events, from gigs to comedy, theatre, street-food markets and all manner of pop-ups.
67 Greenland Street, T 708 2890, www.campandfurnace.com

030

14.30 FACT
Liverpool's Foundation for Art and Creative Technology, a complex of film screens and exhibition spaces championing new media and digital art, is unique within the UK. Architects Austin-Smith:Lord employed a smart playfulness that matches FACT's innovative programming and policy of community involvement through projects such as ARtSENSE, Healthy Spaces and Tenantspin. Exterior zinc tiles evoke giant pixels and the canyon-like interior is shaped by the curved undersides of the screening rooms. The building operates as an internal street; a dynamic necessitated by its hemmed-in footprint, but also to allow engagement with the Ropewalks district, the regeneration of which FACT helped to drive. The outside-in aesthetic is echoed in the materials: polished concrete floors and panels of oxidised steel.
88 Wood Street, T 707 4464,
www.fact.co.uk

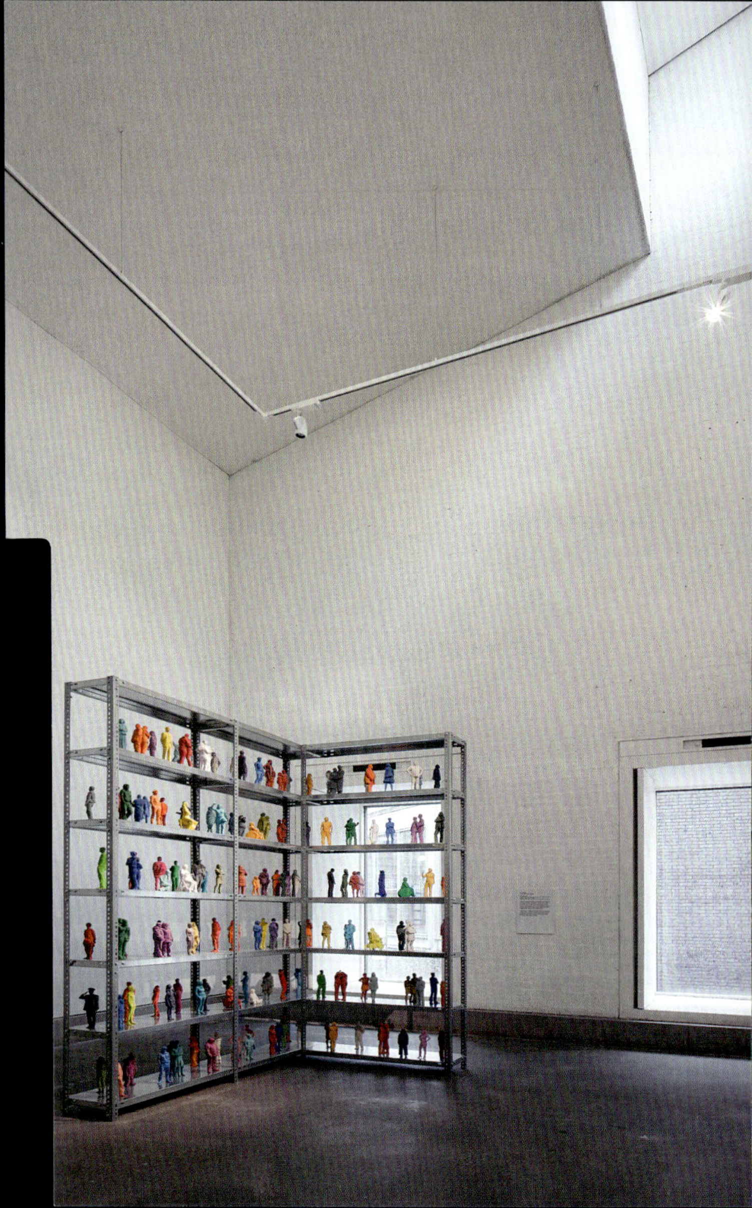

15.30 The Bluecoat

This is the city's oldest building, founded in 1708 as a charity school. The Bluecoat's 'creative hub' label doesn't do full justice to its heritage – in a seminal 1911 show, Roger Fry lined up works by Picasso, Cézanne and Matisse beside Liverpudlian artists; Yoko Ono performed here in 1967; and the institution commissioned Jeremy Deller's *Acid Brass* project in 1996. The Bluecoat also hosts dance, music and literature events, and its cobbled courtyard is lined with craft shops (see p081). A £14m wing by Dutch architects Biq was added in 2008 to expand the exhibition space, which has hosted the likes of 'Museum Visitors 1:8' by Karin Sander (opposite). The garden is a precious oasis and the upstairs bistro a fine spot for an afternoon drink.
School Lane, T 702 5324,
www.thebluecoat.org.uk

17.00 Anglican Cathedral
It's hard to believe, but Lutyens' Catholic cathedral (see p012) would have dwarfed the Anglican. Yet it never came to be, and Giles Gilbert Scott's first commission (he was 22) is still one of the largest churches in the world. Built using sandstone from Woolton, construction dragged on from 1904 until 1978, 18 years after Scott died. Like his 1933 Battersea Power Station, its magnitude can be hard to take in, seeming almost to warp the space around it. The church is curated inventively – look out for Elisabeth Frink's *The Welcoming Christ* above the west entrance, Tracey Emin's *For You* scrawled in pink neon above the west porch and her tiny *Liver Bird* sitting outside on a pole in front of the oratory. Climb up to the 101m tower, ideally a little before sunset, for views as far as the Pennines, Blackpool and the Welsh hills.
St James' Mount, T 709 6271,
www.liverpoolcathedral.org.uk

24 HOURS

19.00 Philharmonic Hall
Herbert J Rowse's Phil opened in 1939, its streamline moderne exterior notable for the stair turrets that resemble a ship's funnel. The auditorium (pictured) features Edmund C Thompson's female figures and its walls seem to ripple like sound waves. Renowned for its acoustics, it hosts concerts, gigs and films, which are preceded by a live organ recital.
Hope Street, T 709 3789

24 HOURS

22.00 Panoramic 34
The water views from this birds' nest eyrie are reminiscent of Chicago's Signature Room or Toronto's 360. Liverpool's last attempt at such a venue was the revolving restaurant in St John's Beacon that closed some 30 years ago. Architects R2A wanted to evoke a mid-20th-century feel; panelling apes the cabins of the cruise ships that sailed down the Mersey. The space opened in 2008 when the city was heady with its own potential. Liverpool service can be overly pally, but here it's butler-discreet. Less smooth is a menu described as 'innovative British' that features foie gras, chorizo and falafel. Still, chef Parth Bhatt's tasting selection is one of the finest in town and, served Tuesday to Thursday only, a reason to prolong the weekend break.
34th floor, West Tower, 10 Brook Street, T 236 5534, www.panoramicliverpool.com

23.30 81LTD/Salt Dog Slims

Secreted away in a Georgian terrace, Salt Dog Slims is a US-style sports/dive bar that takes its beer seriously, serving 24 bottled varieties plus draught in tankards and steins. The menu sticks to sausages in buns but the chilli dog is the real deal — topped with shin of beef and spiced with cumin, coriander and paprika. However, there is a surprise in store — ask at the bar for the code and head up to the speakeasy 81LTD (above). It's a laidback space with a walnut bar, leather banquettes, bare brick walls and a pressed-tin ceiling. Here, cocktails are king and homemade bitters and spirit infusions are used to create concoctions like camomile rye whisky and walnut rum. An alternative late-night haunt is the slice of Mexicana on Slater Street (see p051).
79-83 Seel Street, T 709 7172,
www.saltdogslims.co.uk

URBAN LIFE
CAFÉS, RESTAURANTS, BARS AND NIGHTCLUBS

Ever since Liverpool welcomed the first sailors on shore leave, it has been a good-time city. In The Cavern in the 1960s and Cream in the 1990s, it had world-famous, era-defining venues too, and a few, such as The Magnet (see p044), are still going strong. However, these days club promoters chime with the zeitgeist by running pop-up nights. Look out for house-oriented Chibuku and Circus, parties by *Waxxx* magazine, often held at Camp and Furnace (see p028), and gigs put on by Deep Hedonia and Evol. A lively gay scene centres on the twin nodes of G-Bar (1-7 Eberle Street, T 236 4416) and Superstar Boudoir (24 Stanley Street).

The city has always been concerned more with hedonism than sophistication, yet the culinary movement has evolved organically and is reaching heady heights of its own as chefs raid the north-west's natural larder to create modern British menus. As well as our featured venues, try The Side Door (29a Hope Street, T 707 7888), Spire (1 Church Road, T 734 5040) and Puschka (16 Rodney Street, T 708 8698). For refined drinks, the cocktail scene centres mainly on hotels, in the White Bar at the Radisson Blu (see p016) and Bar Four at Hard Days Night (see p020). The eye-smacking Blacksheep-designed Playground club (see p016), with its faceted mirrors, crushed velvet and label hell, provides a glimpse of the city at its sassiest – or most ridiculous, depending on your mood. *For full addresses, see Resources.*

Merchants Bar & Restaurant

Liverpool architects Lucy and Littler's 1868 Alliance Bank houses the 62 Castle Street hotel and restaurant Merchants. It's located across the road from the Crown Court, and the hotel adopted muted tones with the world-weary judiciary in mind, but it's a tad gloomy for our tastes. The eaterie in the banking hall is another matter. Spherical metallic 'Fort Knox' pendants by Viso cluster beneath a marble dome above the bar. Elsewhere, WIS Design's 'Umbrella' lights hang from the stuccoed ceiling. It's a sultry space after dark, although the mishmash feel of the menu is occasionally reflected in the cooking. However, the chef has a way with batter, from tempura to fish'n'chips, and champions local produce in dishes such as Lancashire cheese soufflé.
56-62 Castle Street, T 702 7897, www.62castlest.com

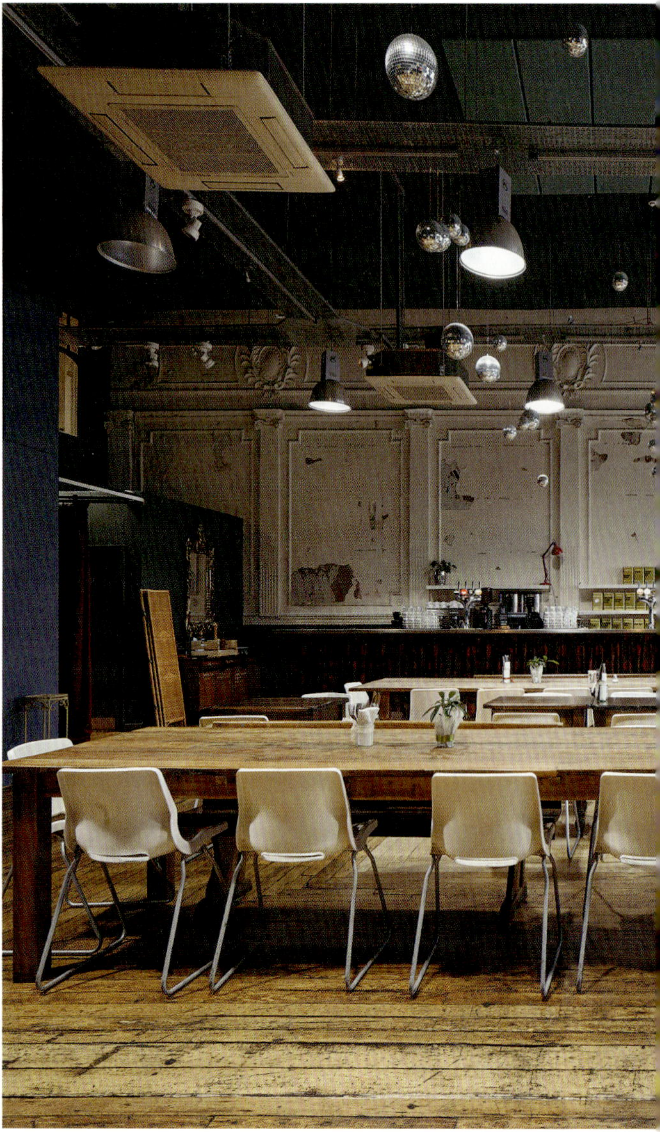

Leaf

Before moving to the city centre proper in 2010, Leaf fine-tuned the model in the Baltic Triangle. How that neighbourhood could now do with a little more of what Leaf is brewing here, because this Bold Street venue is rarely anything less than jam-packed. It works just as well for tea and cake as for beer, events, classes and live music. The art deco facade was installed by a 1930s car dealership, but much of the success of the two-floored venue is thanks to a multi-purpose interior devised by local firms R2A and SB Studio. The place is billed as a 'punk' take on the English tearoom (ironically twee lampshades share ceiling space with disco balls), but really Leaf is neither spit-and-sawdust nor prim-and-proper.
65-67 Bold Street, T 707 7747, www.thisisleaf.co.uk

The Magnet

When nightclub The Sink opened in the cellar of the Rumblin' Tum coffee shop in 1963, its R&B-jazz-blues soundtrack was a counterpoint to The Cavern's Merseybeat. It's been The Magnet since 1998, yet the 1960s spirit endures in artistic director Johnny Mellor's retro focus, from the Vegas pinball-machine tops to the geometric tiling, padded walls, aquarium set into the bar and the logo itself. Music downstairs ranges from one-off sets from the likes of Norman Jay and Roy Ayers to regular DJ nights. It's the only worthwhile city venue with a 24-hour licence, and the 1am to 6am Sunday sessions are a hedonist's dream finish to a weekend. If you want The Sink of old, look out for occasional nights at the Cabin Club (139 Wood Street).
45 Hardman Street, T 709 4000,
www.themagnetliverpool.com

Hanover Street Social

Liverpool ONE injected a new vitality into the city centre. At the junction of Hanover, Duke and Paradise Streets there has been a trio of culinary happenings since 2010: Salt House Tapas (T 706 0092), in the Bishop of Liverpool's former residence, converted by architects Snow; The Hub (T 709 2401), which lives up to its name; and Hanover Street Social. Its warehouse interior, supported by iron girders, is lit courtesy of Tom Dixon, leather banquettes and black-and-white floor tiles lend a diner feel, and original photography hangs on exposed brick walls. This part of town comes into its own in the evenings when the nearby Mersey does a fine line in sunsets, which are perfect with oysters, dressed crab or something off the grill.
Casartelli Building, 16-20 Hanover Street, T 709 8784, www.hanoverstreetsocial.co.uk

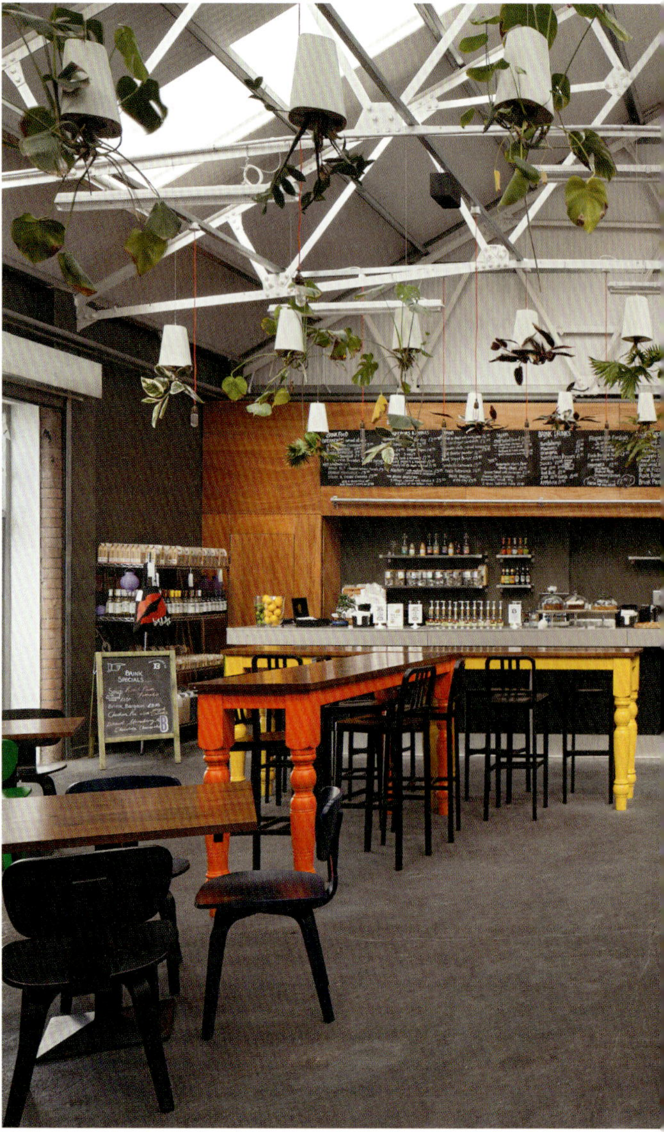
BANK
SPECIALS

The Brink
The city's only dry bar provides solace and excellent mocktails for recovering addicts. R2A and SB Studio combined to transform a garage into an uplifting, airy space decorated with 'sky planters' and wood panels laser-cut with witty slogans. The sun-trap patio and comfort-food lunch menu have helped turn The Brink into a heart-warming success.
15-21 Parr Street, T 703 0582

URBAN LIFE

Waterhouse Cafe

Many of the city's cultural institutions have their own eateries. Our favourites are the Welsford in the Anglican Cathedral (see p034) and this spot in the Victoria Gallery & Museum. The building was completed in 1892 to the neo-Gothic design of Alfred Waterhouse, and went on to house the HQ of the University of Liverpool, giving rise to the term 'red-brick university', before becoming a museum in 2008. Head to the first floor to see work by William Turner, Jacob Epstein, Elisabeth Frink and Lucian Freud. Its double-height café is partly lined with Burmantofts terracotta and features a huge fireplace. It's only open during the day, so come for lunch – perhaps try local speciality 'scouse', an Irish stew-like dish served with red cabbage – or a cream tea.
Victoria Gallery & Museum, Ashton Street, T 795 0333, www.liv.ac.uk/vgm/cafe

Philharmonic Dining Rooms

Walter Thomas' busy interior was a revolt against the Georgian simplicity nearby. It opened in 1900 as a fancy watering hole for theatregoers from the Philharmonic Hall (see p036). In a riot of art nouveau, there are mosaic floors, elaborate wood carvings, Corinthian pillars, stained glass and ceramic tiles, and musical motifs abound inside and out. Parapets, turrets, balconies and an oriel window bulging like a beer keg give it a watchful presence and it became a city icon. Indeed, Lennon was said to have lamented not being able to pop by this grand boozer once he became famous. It serves a fine selection of real ale and decent pub grub. Men should not be alarmed to find the opposite sex in the toilet – the roseate marble urinals are the city's oddest sightseeing stop.
36 Hope Street, T 707 2837

050

Studio2

Cobbled, rough-around-the-edges Parr Street has long attracted the city's hippest venues; the surrounding area is home to The Kazimier (overleaf) and tequila joints Santa Chupitos and El Bandito (T 707 6527). Then there's this recording studio/bar/hotel complex. Three of the studios are still operational and another two now mix drinks rather than sounds. Studio2 is the most interesting, with bass traps above the bar where a mixing desk once sat and original features like mic inputs, speakers and stone walls, with shabby-chic seats and armchairs scattered about. The highlight of the diverse programme is Tuesday's ParrJazz. If you have a few too many, you could do worse than stay the night here. On the second floor is a 12-room budget boutique (T 707 1050) with a penthouse annexe round the corner in Argyle Street.
33-45 Parr Street, T 707 3727,
www.parrstreet.co.uk

The Kazimier

Wolstenholme Square was home to Nation and its iconic Cream night. The Kazimier opened here in 2008, reviving the tradition of crackpot, quasi-mystical Scouse antics with immersive, theatrical happenings. The Kaz has since shifted towards straight live music — The xx, The Magic Band, Metronomy and Jonathan Richman have taken to the stage — but contemporary dance and experiential theatre still form part of the edgy programme. This is aided and abetted by the octagonal form of the venue, which has a kind of skewed art deco feel, with white-on-black graphics. Outside, Cuban Jorge Pardo's striking sculpture of colourful car-sized spheres suspended on stalks was created for the 2006 biennial and symbolises the ropemaking industry.
4-5 Wolstenholme Square, T 324 1723, www.thekazimier.co.uk

Maya

Aztec goddess Mayahuel is associated with the agave plant, and tequila worship is very much the order of the day here. There's a line-up of shots called Zapatistas and cocktails inspired by the imagery of the Mexican bingo game Lotería. Try the Santa Muerte, with its blood-coloured ice ball, or El Diablito, made with sotol as opposed to tequila, or a simple sipping mescal. The gothic feel of the vaulted cellar has been cranked up a notch or two in homage to Mexico's Day of the Dead, and neon crucifixes and naked bulbs in cages glow starkly. Upstairs eaterie Lucha Libre is purposely bright and breezy in order to foster a street-versus-underworld contrast. Head chef Luis Michel hails from Guadalajara and his signature slow-cooked lamb dish, *birria*, is typical of Jalisco.
96 Wood Street, T 329 0200

The Warehouse Kitchen + Bar
Southport, 32km north of Liverpool, was built on recreation not industry and is a town of retirement homes and ice-cream parlours. The Warehouse, which has stylish interiors by Design LSM, is where to head for dinner by the sea — try the Southport shrimp or Formby asparagus from the locally sourced menu.
30 West Street, T 01704 544 662,
www.warehousekitchenandbar.com

URBAN LIFE

Fraiche

Although chef Marc Wilkinson cooks for just five tables in a converted mid-19th-century terraced house in villagey Oxton, he hasn't escaped the notice of Michelin, which awarded Fraiche a star in 2009. The three tasting menus have French roots, and his signatures are temperature shifts and bold flavours; we'd rush back for the sherry-poached cockles with *yuzu* jelly and courgette alone. The decor has a subtle coastal theme. Jenny Barker created the seaweed-inspired glasswork – her pieces are sold by The Bluecoat (see p081) – and the 'Styrene' pendant lights made from heat-shrunken coffee cups (flotsam and jetsam repurposed) are by Londoner Paul Cocksedge. Stop off for a pre-dinner drink in Oxton Bar & Kitchen (T 651 2535).
11 Rose Mount, T 652 2914,
www.restaurantfraiche.com

MPW Steakhouse

Falconer Chester Hall and Manchester studio Carroll Design's blueprint for the Marco Pierre White franchise in Hotel Indigo riffs on a thread motif symbolising the cotton trade. Lampshades resemble cotton balls and a bold yellow scheme evokes the sunshine that fuels the crop. Chef Chris Jones takes the reins, but MPW dictates the menu and occasionally drops by to ensure justice is done to signature dishes like Billy By potage of mussels and Wally Ladd sherry trifle. The 28-day aged steaks are cut from Flintshire cattle and served with beef-dripping chips, and other local produce includes Fleetwood fish and Inglewhite cheese; beer, cider and tea are sourced from the area too. At the bar, try the cotton martini, poured over candyfloss.
Hotel Indigo, 10 Chapel Street, T 559 0555, www.mpwsteakhouseliverpool.co.uk

60 Hope Street

One of the city's prime addresses, Hope Street in the Georgian Quarter is lined with cultural venues and bookended by cathedrals. At No 60, a townhouse has been converted into smart dining rooms; walls were ripped out to open up the space, and Eames-inspired furniture, Artemide lighting and oak floors were introduced. Chef Damian Flynn's cuisine offers hints of haute cuisine, but also a heartiness and playfulness exemplified by the signature fish battered in local Cains beer and a deep-fried jam sandwich. On the same street, in Hope Street Hotel (see p018), Paul Askew's cooking at London Carriage Works (T 705 2222) is highly accomplished. The restaurant features canvases by poet and painter Adrian Henri, who lived nearby.
60 Hope Street, T 707 6060,
www.60hopestreet.com

The Lawns
Foodies will find themselves drawn across the river to the Wirral. As well as Fraiche (see p056), there's Nova (T 342 9959), Da Piero (T 648 7373), Peninsula Dining Room (T 639 8338) and The Lawns, which has a charming rural setting barely 20 minutes out of the tunnel. Chef David Gillmore's button-pushing menus have seen the restaurant's star rise quickly since 2010; mains of rose veal with sweetbread ravioli, and Aberdaron crab with courgette flower and tomato sorbet showcase his focus on imaginatively prepared local ingredients. The restaurant's original mid-19th-century features include oak carvings, a ceiling embossed with mother of pearl and a neoclassical bas relief. The attached Thornton Hall Hotel has a lovely spa.
Neston Road, Thornton Hough, T 336 3938, www.lawnsrestaurant.co.uk

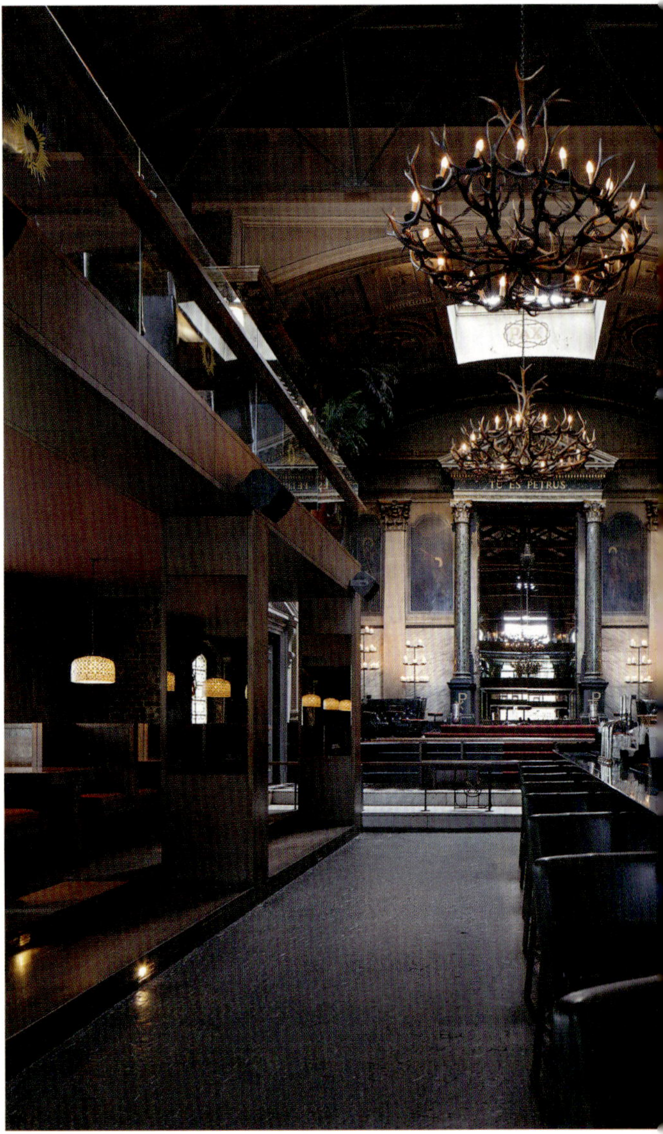
PAX
TU ES PETRUS

Alma de Cuba

This is the oldest religious building in the city centre, serving as St Peter's Church from 1788. Urban Splash took it over in 2004, envisaging an office conversion, but it finally opened as this bar/restaurant with a loose Latino theme – witness the fake palm trees. Such a use hardly seems respectful, but it did save the site. The captivating altar remains and is joined by religious relics, such as stations of the cross and a harmonium, recovered from a vault in the Metropolitan Cathedral. More bizarrely, chandeliers made of antlers hang from the barn-like roof. The mezzanine serves as a restaurant, but the global menu isn't much to write home about. Carnival dancers work the space at weekends when it's de rigueur to dress up to the nines; rather brilliantly, Sunday brunch is accompanied by a gospel choir.
St Peter's Church, Seel Street, T 702 7394, www.alma-de-cuba.com

INSIDER'S GUIDE
JACQUELINE PASSMORE, FILM DIRECTOR AND ARTIST

Texan Jacqueline Passmore has made Liverpool her home since 2003 and lives in Sefton Park. Her large-scale film installations have been exhibited in the ICA and the Tate Modern, she creates live video mixes for the likes of Stereolab and lectures at LJMU's School of Art and Design (see p073). 'The city has an independent spirit where radical movements are allowed to thrive,' she says.

Passmore likes to kick off her day at Bold Street Coffee (89 Bold Street, T 707 0760) before a browse in The Vinyl Emporium (124 Bold Street) or the institution that is Probe Records (School Lane, T 708 8815): 'Liverpool's all about music.' She describes design store Cow&Co (15 Cleveland Square, T 0844 858 1581) as 'total eye candy' and also loves Raiders Vintage (38 Renshaw Street, T 709 2929). After lunch and a visit to the gourmet deli at Delifonseca (12 Stanley Street, T 255 0808), Passmore checks to see what's on at Wolstenholme Creative Space (11 Wolstenholme Square). 'There are so many exciting artists here, such as the painter Cherie Grist.'

For dinner, she suggests tapas at Catalonian fusion restaurant Lunya (18-20 College Lane, T 706 9770), where there are more than 100 dishes on the menu, before heading to a pub like Roscoe Head (24 Roscoe Street, T 709 4365) to soak up the community spirit. Her top late-night haunt is The Kazimier (see p052). 'It's a porthole to a bohemian wonderland; 1930s Paris meets the Mersey. Beautiful.'
For full addresses, see Resources.

URBAN LIFE

ARCHITOUR
A GUIDE TO LIVERPOOL'S ICONIC BUILDINGS

Liverpool's buildings tell a story of rise, decline and regeneration. The port grew thanks to a world-first engineering marvel. Thomas Steers' 1715 enclosed commercial dock meant ships could unload whatever the tides were doing. With pleasing historical circularity, Liverpool ONE (see p078), the 21st-century sheen of rebirth, sits on top of it. Jesse Hartley's dock engineering is mostly intact and the mid-19th- to early 20th-century prosperity it created remains superbly illustrated in the Pier Head (see p026) and Herbert J Rowse's financial institutions Martins Bank (4 Water Street) and India Buildings (Water Street), both from 1932. Charles Herbert Reilly's Liverpool School of Architecture was hugely influential in this period and for decades to come, its graduates producing some outstanding eccentricities, such as St Monica's Church (see p069).

Since the onset of decline in the 1970s, reuse has been of a higher quality than new-builds. Albert Dock was pioneering, transformed in the late 1980s into a leisure hub boasting James Stirling's Tate Liverpool (T 702 7400); elsewhere, developer Urban Splash and architect partners shedkm converted every warehouse they could get their hands on. While such gentrification continues, the city is now also looking skywards as it seeks to reassert its clout; if it goes ahead, Maurice Shapero's 199m shipping-container-inspired King Edwards Tower will be the UK's tallest structure outside London. *For full addresses, see Resources.*

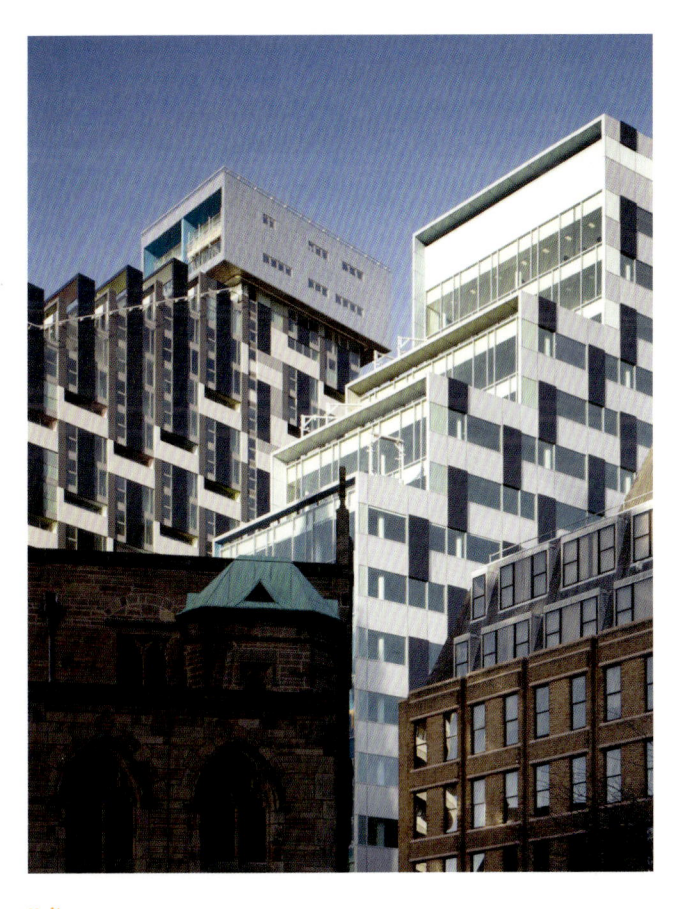

Unity

AHMM's design for the cladding on Unity's RIBA-award-winning twin riverside towers was inspired by 'dazzle' camouflage – the bold, clashing geometric shapes painted on ships that were docked in the harbour during WWI. Lead architect Paul Monaghan also slipped in his mother's name in Morse code. The residential block rises in steps up to 86m and is topped by a penthouse that locals refer to as the 'portacabin', and the smaller commercial tower was Liverpool's first purpose-built office block for 30 years. The 2006 complex descends like icebergs on the down-on-its-luck Thistle Hotel, forming a motley trio with The Capital (see p068) and Queensway Tunnel ventilation tower (see p072) – the boxy structures seeming to jostle each other in a bid to dominate this part of town.
3 Rumford Place

Active Learning Lab
Architects Sheppard Robson drafted in Arup's lighting team for the University of Liverpool's 2009 engineering facility. Seeming to hover above a 1960s block, the cantilevered oblong is faced with LED panels that colour-shift to create patterns and messages. At night, as the kaleidoscopic exterior pulses, there's something *Close Encounters* about it.
Brownlow Hill

ARCHITOUR

The Capital

Like the Royal Liver Building (see p026), near-neighbour The Capital was also built for an insurance company and apes its grandiose scale, but it's nowhere near as well loved. Finished in 1976 as the HQ for Royal Insurance (later Royal & Sun Alliance), local wariness can be attributed to Tripe & Wakeham's brutalist approach; rumours of a recladding to mask the brown concrete might improve its profile. Some know it with a degree of fondness as the 'sandcastle', but there's a touch of the mountainside lair about its 13 storeys. The narrow windows contribute much to that, although they're one of its most impressive features in functional terms (they conserve energy). The current name was bestowed by developer Downing, which bought the building in 2006 and leases office space.
New Hall Place

St Monica's Church

Francis Xavier Velarde, the designer of this 1936 Catholic church, was a star alumnus of Liverpool School of Architecture. His rectilinear brick modernist church was pioneering in the UK, although it shows the influence of 1920s and 1930s continental ecclesiastical architecture (particularly the work of German Dominikus Böhm). The repetition of the neatly punched slender windows first catches the eye, but Herbert Tyson Smith's three angels are its best-known feature. Looking like skittles or dolly pegs from a distance, they seem to peer down their noses when you stand below. Smith was the most influential sculptor of the period. He contributed to Martins Bank (see p064) — see the bronze doors — but his greatest work is the reliefs on the 1930 Cenotaph by St George's Hall (see p009).
Fernhill Road, T 922 4819

Port Sunlight
A century before Liverpool ONE (see p078) came this masterpiece of town planning. The model village was devised to house Bolton-born industrialist William Hesketh Lever's soap-factory (the 'Sunlight' brand) workers in an environment that exemplified garden city and Arts and Crafts aesthetics. The majority of housing was built between 1899 and 1914. For diversity, Lever brought in 30 different practices, many from the north-west, including his ally Charles Herbert Reilly, who designed 15-27 Lower Road (pictured). Among the London architects were Maurice Adams, Ernest Newton and Edwin Lutyens, who was responsible for 17-23 Corniche Road. The best of Port Sunlight's public buildings is the 1922 neoclassical Lady Lever Art Gallery on Lower Road (T 478 4136) by William & Segar Owen, the most prolific architects here.

071

ARCHITOUR

St George's Dock Ventilation Tower

In his work on the Mersey tunnel system, Herbert J Rowse embraced art deco as he celebrated man's technological progress in his architecture, notably in this towering ventilation shaft and command station above the Queensway entrance. The 1934 Portland stone-faced obelisk is decorated with sculptures by Edmund Thompson and George Capstick, including two basalt figures, *Night and Day* (the tunnel never closes), and *Speed*, a stylised motorbike-rider. The interior houses offices (hardly used) and huge ventilation fans, and tours can be arranged. Also look out for Rowse's 1934 ventilation tower at Woodside (see p025) and the rocket-like shafts of the Kingsway tunnel, built in 1971, designed by Bradshaw, Rowse & Harker.
*The Strand, T 227 5181,
www.merseytunnels.co.uk*

Art and Design Academy

The Active Learning Lab (see p066) serves as a dynamic advert for the University of Liverpool, and this 2009 building by Rick Mather Architects achieves the same for John Moores University's art and design faculty. The school dates back to 1825 and had amassed disparate premises across the city, including the one in Mount Street where John Lennon, Isabel Rawsthorne and Bill Harry studied. This £24m site united the department and won a RIBA award. The serpentine design tucks in neatly alongside its circular neighbour, the Metropolitan Cathedral (see p012). There are further reverberations – tiered roof terraces evoke Gibberd's piazza and light-maximising, splayed studio windows mimic the church's segmented design.
Brownlow Hill, T 904 1216,
www.ljmu.ac.uk/lsa

Oriel Chambers

It is astonishing that Peter Ellis' groundbreaking Oriel Chambers was unveiled as far back as 1864; its use of iron-framed curtain walling would see large-scale expression in US skyscrapers two decades later. The office building used to extend further up Covent Garden, but was bombed in WWII. The oriel windows allowed in light but their shape was not the innovation; rather it's the way they're hung on the core. The sandstone, too, is largely decorative. The cast-iron courtyard staircase encased in glazing is said to have inspired Chicago School architect John Root. Yet, locally, Oriel Chambers was widely derided at the time, and such criticism might explain why there's only one other building known to be by Ellis, at 16 Cook Street, before he renounced architecture altogether.
14 Water Street

Heroes of the Marine Engine Room

Welsh sculptor William Goscombe John's naturalistic portrayal of the engine room heroes who perished with the Titanic and during WWI is the highlight of this 1916 memorial, which chimes with the city's championing of the working man. Of course, those making a living at sea are even closer to Scouse hearts. The tribute was originally intended to mark only the deaths on the Titanic – a ship built in Belfast for the Liverpool-based White Star Line (see p009) – but its scope was widened with the Great War. The figures are the most remarkable element of the 14.6m granite obelisk, which is topped by a gilded flame. It is strikingly modernist in comparison to John's other Liverpool work, of which the most interesting is his 1921 WWI memorial in Port Sunlight (see p070).
St Nicholas Place

Sefton Park Palm House

The 95-hectare Sefton Park opened in 1872. A collaboration between local Lewis Hornblower and Édouard André (*jardinier principal* for Paris), its arcing paths are laid out in an informal network and meet obliquely, making the park seem larger. The gothic entrance gates are a fine contrast to the Palm House, a 25m-high octagonal dome of 3,710 glass panes by Scottish architects Mackenzie and Moncur, which was finished in 1896 (it was rebuilt in 2001). Eight statues by Léon-Joseph Chavailliaud stand outside, depicting figures of horticulture and exploration. The park was financed by the sale of plots on its periphery – most interesting are the gothic towers of the 1874 Rankin Hall on Ullet Road. Nearby Lark Lane is a hive of pubs and eateries.
T 726 9304, www.palmhouse.org.uk

ARCHITOUR

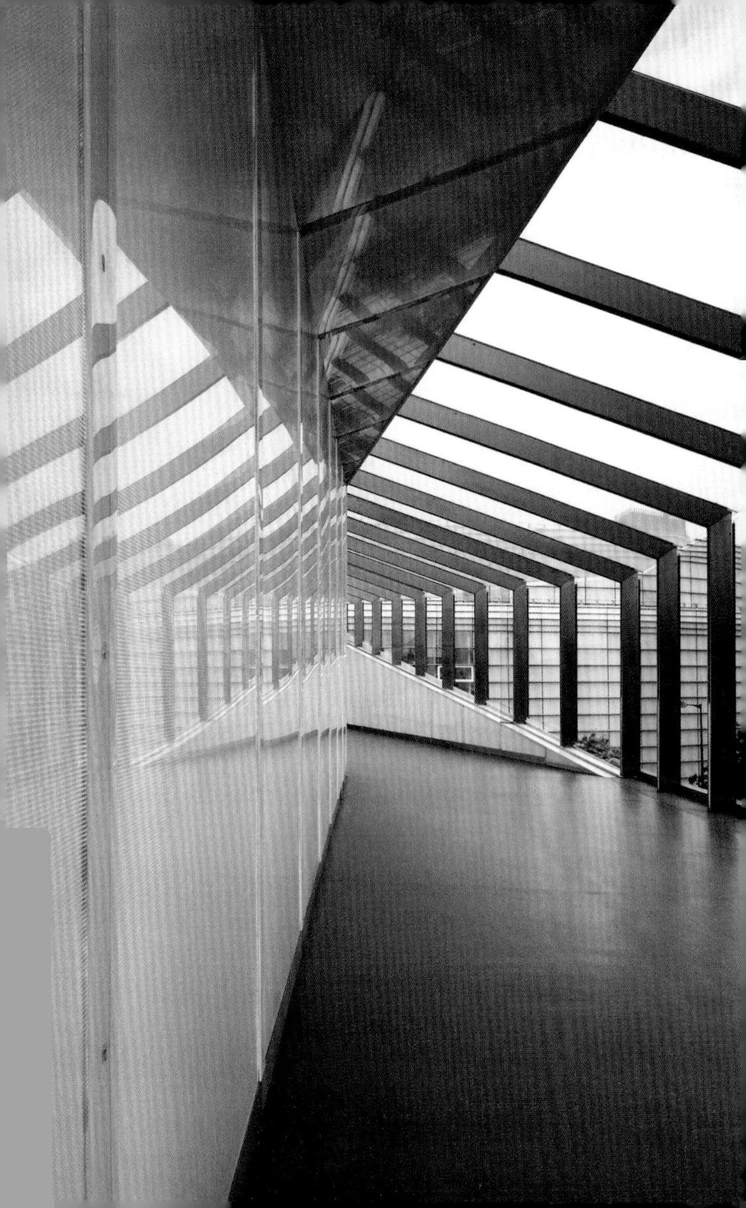

Liverpool ONE Footbridge

Property developer Grosvenor showed nerve in securing 17 hectares of prime land on a 250-year lease. Architects BDP matched it with the Liverpool ONE masterplan, which in 2009 was the first ever to be shortlisted for a RIBA Stirling Prize, drafting in 26 firms to design some 40 buildings to revive these ailing streets. Far more than a shopping complex, it has rewired the city centre, providing new pedestrian routes and perspectives. Wilkinson Eyre's 60m-span bridge at the Paradise Street interchange (above) is just one of them. Constructed of steel plate and glass, it seems to twist as you walk beneath it. It's appropriate that one of Liverpool ONE's most stylish structures points towards the Baltic Triangle, the city district most in need of increased footfall.
Paradise Street/Hanover Street

SHOPPING
THE BEST RETAIL THERAPY AND WHAT TO BUY

Due to its trade links and great warehouses, Liverpool fancied itself as the British Empire's very own emporium. In the 1865 Compton House on Church Street (now M&S), it had arguably the world's first department store. Gerald de Courcy Fraser's later Lewis's has been sliced up for development, but was an icon with an influence that extended far beyond Liverpool. But economic woes hit, and the city's popularity as a retail destination plummeted in the 1980s.

Liverpool ONE has reversed that trend, although it's primarily a purveyor of big brands and well-known retailers. Scouse fashion is notoriously a law unto itself – long-standing proponents of the 'colourful' style are Cricket (9 Cavern Walks, T 227 4645) and its cheekier little sister Boudoir Boutique (14 Cavern Walks, T 231 1424). Bold Street was once the North's version of Bond Street but now has an edgy appeal as a hub of independents, from bookstore News From Nowhere (No 96, T 708 7270) to Utility (see p086).

The city is far stronger on crafts. Seek out leatherworkers Nook & Willow (36 Seel Street, T 708 5576), design-led homewares at Cow&Co (see p062) and Alison Appleton's ceramics at Made Here (Metquarter, T 07956 852 331). A great one-stop shopping venue is The Bluecoat courtyard (see p032), where you'll find handmade pieces at Landbaby (T 07504 479 440) and the cyanotype prints of Donald Short at architecturally focused Blueprint (T 709 5297). *For full addresses, see Resources.*

The Bluecoat Display Centre
Established in 1959, the Display Centre is the oldest tenant at The Bluecoat (see p032) and one of the UK's earliest craft galleries. It looks out on to Liverpool ONE, yet this unique shop was never likely to be threatened by the spread of a retail giant. University professor and architect Robert Gardner-Medwin set it up to support designers whose work he admired and, of course, to provide home-enhancing pieces. These days, more than 350 contemporary applied artists are represented in the store. Look out for Sue Binns' ceramics (Butter Dome, above, £84), local metalworker Rebecca Gouldson's pieces and Michael Brennand-Wood's mixed-media and textile creations; retail activity is complemented by a rotating exhibition programme.
College Lane, T 709 4014,
www.bluecoatdisplaycentre.com

Static Gallery

There's a hands-on ethic to this gallery set within another former factory, in which simple timber construction is used for easy manipulation of the space. The interior comprises a café, 10 glass-fronted studio units (Imogen Stidworthy is a resident) and an exhibition space – highlights have included 'Damien Hirst: One Night Only' and 'Terminal Convention' (*We Close Our Eyes* video installation by gallery director Paul Sullivan, above). It used to host gigs until a noise abatement order in 2012, so instead Static concentrated on operating as a commercial gallery – a timely move given that the city had lost its finest when Ceri Hand defected to the capital. In south Liverpool, Corke Art Gallery (T 726 0232) is worth a detour from Sefton Park.
23 Roscoe Lane, T 707 0770,
www.statictrading.com

SHOPPING

Weavers Door

The local love of continental sportswear and chunky logos began with the football casual in the 1970s and was further stoked by iconic store Wade Smith, but the arrival of Weavers Door has ushered Liverpudlian men in another direction. The focus is on heritage brands with functional aesthetics and an emphasis on craftsmanship and durability. Many labels are from the UK, US and Scandinavia, and include Fjällräven, Penfield, Universal Works, Oliver Spencer, Folk and Norse Projects, plus shoes from Grenson and Red Wing. Interiors have an appropriately vintage feel, and there's a pop-up barber once a month. It's a smart choice of location for a menswear store as Cavern Walks was the stamping ground for the city's hipsters in the 1950s and 1960s.
1 Cavern Walks, Harrington Street, T 236 6001, www.weaversdoor.com

Benna

Central Saint Martins graduate and fashion stylist Benna Harry launched her jewellery emporium online before converting this basement to personally offer clients the benefit of her discerning eye. Harry has a knack of picking up lines before they come on trend. Stocking Shorouk was one coup, as was snapping up Annina Vogel's reworked vintage before Kate Moss gave her seal of approval. More high-end statement pieces come courtesy of Lara Bohinc, Sydney Evan and Erickson Beamon; also worth seeking out are Anton Heunis, Mawi and Kismet by Milka. The showroom, with its Victorian-era display cabinets, bell jars and glass boxes, and antique flower wall lights, defers to the history of the area. By appointment only.
Rodney Street, T 0845 872 0899, www.benna.co.uk

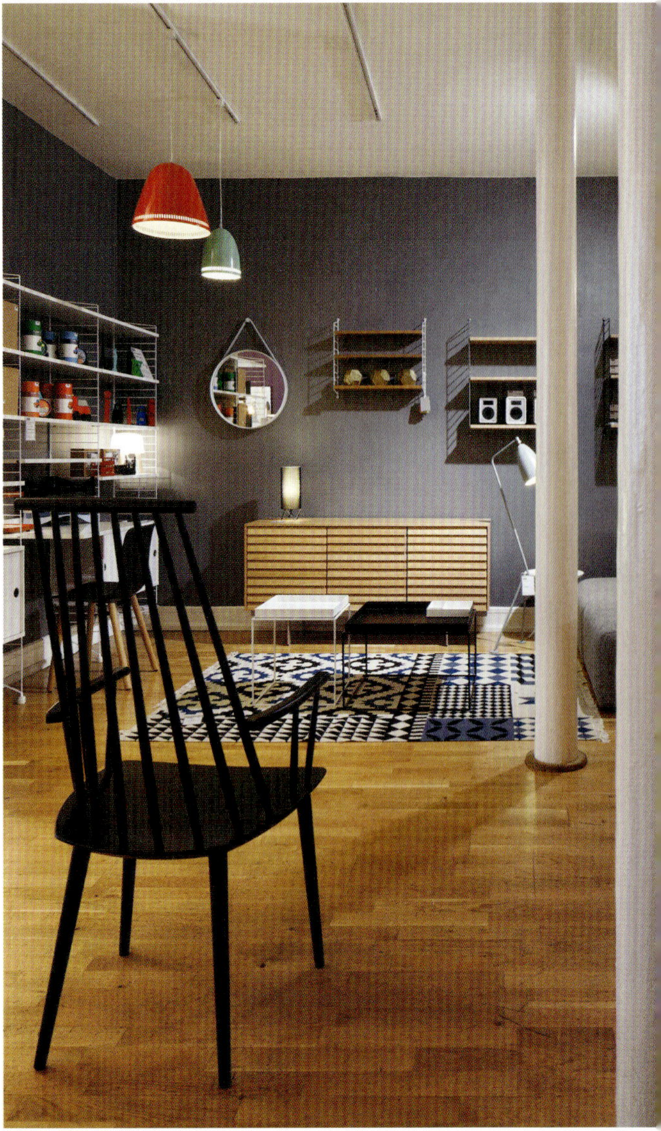

Utility

The design-led products at Utility have proved a hit since the shop opened in 1999. Its homewares range set European names alongside independent makers, and was quickly followed by high-end furniture and lighting, as one store became two, then three, plus another in London. The original address at 86 Bold Street (T 707 9919) is now gift-focused, whereas the one at No 60 (left) sells pieces by top designers, from Thomas Heatherwick to Konstantin Grcic, Tom Dixon, Matthew Hilton, Yngve Ekström and Lee Broom. Utility also stocks its own range of kitchenware and leather goods, including briefcases and satchels made in nearby Knowsley. Look, too, for vintage classics such as the elegantly functional Tala Cook's Dry Measure, which has been produced in a Bootle metal factory since the 1920s.
60 Bold Street, T 708 4192, www.utilitydesign.co.uk

SPORTS AND SPAS
WORK OUT, CHILL OUT OR JUST WATCH

The city's football heavyweights – Liverpool and Everton – have a decorated past and remain two of the Premier League's top sides, their grounds separated only by Stanley Park. For an insight into the Scouse psyche, derby clashes are unmissable; both clubs also offer stadium tours. The Oval Leisure Centre (Old Chester Road, T 606 2010) in Bebington, not far from Port Sunlight, is where the Olympic scenes from *Chariots of Fire* were shot. For a more central jogging route, pound the 5km waterfront stretch from Albert Dock to Otterspool Promenade, or make for the southern parks – Sefton (see p076) and Calderstones, with its famous megaliths.

The most aesthetically pleasing pool in town is Denys Lasdun's brutalist 1966 University Sports and Fitness Centre (Peach Street, T 794 3307), which has been renovated recently. If the weather's favourable, get out in the elements. Liverpool Watersports Centre (110 Mariners Wharf, T 708 9322) offers canoe tours of Albert Dock and more. Further north is Owen Ellis Architects' sleek glass-and-wood Crosby Lakeside Adventure Centre (Cambridge Road, T 966 6868), which is strong on windsurfing and sailing. Close by here is sculptor Antony Gormley's ethereal *Another Place* – 100 life-sized iron men spread out across the beach, the tide rising and falling around them. Further round the coast and backed by sand dunes, Freshfield Beach is a beautiful spot to go for a dip yourself. *For full addresses, see Resources.*

Awesome Walls
The north docks boast some of the city's most striking structures, and the sight of its ventilation shafts and the Tate & Lyle Silo (see p009) will have climbers reaching for the chalk powder. Satisfy the craving at nearby Awesome Walls inside St Albans Church, which dates from 1849. There's a 17.5m main wall with an 8m overhang; scale it by either top-roping, lead climbing or dry-tooling. The centre hosts national competitions and organises the somewhat surreal annual abseiling event down the Anglican Cathedral (see p034). Those with more of a bouldering focus should try the huge Climbing Hangar (T 345 0587). Outdoor types head to Pex Hill in Cronton, Irby Quarry on the Wirral and, of course, Snowdon in north Wales.
St Albans Church, Athol Street, T 298 2422, www.awesomewalls.co.uk

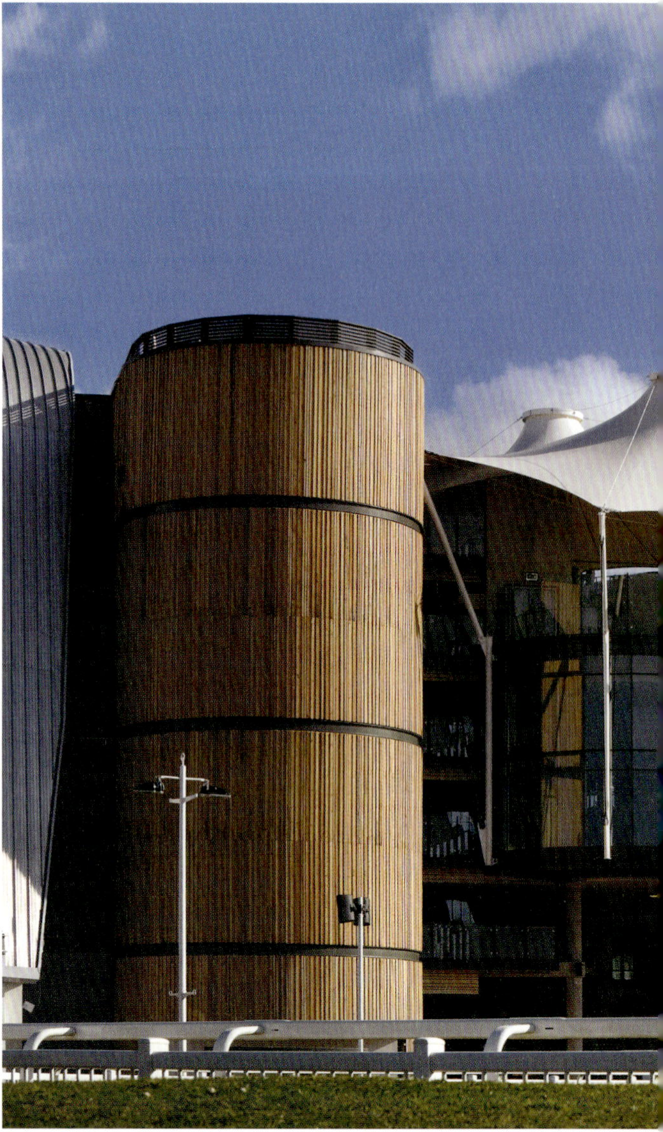

Aintree

The status of Aintree as one of the world's most celebrated racecourses is thanks to just one 10-minute race each year – the Grand National steeplechase, run here since 1839 on land originally leased from Lord Sefton. Even if it's primarily a TV event, the facilities were unworthy of the race's magnitude before BDP's £34m redevelopment, completed in 2007. The two new grandstands accommodate 6,600 spectators and are zinc-clad with trellising for climbing plants. In silhouette, the cantilevered roofs are designed to resemble the peak of a jockey's cap. The Saddle Bar pavilion links the stands, and affords views of a new parade ring, positioned with the early April sun in mind.
Ormskirk Road, T 523 2600, www.aintree.co.uk

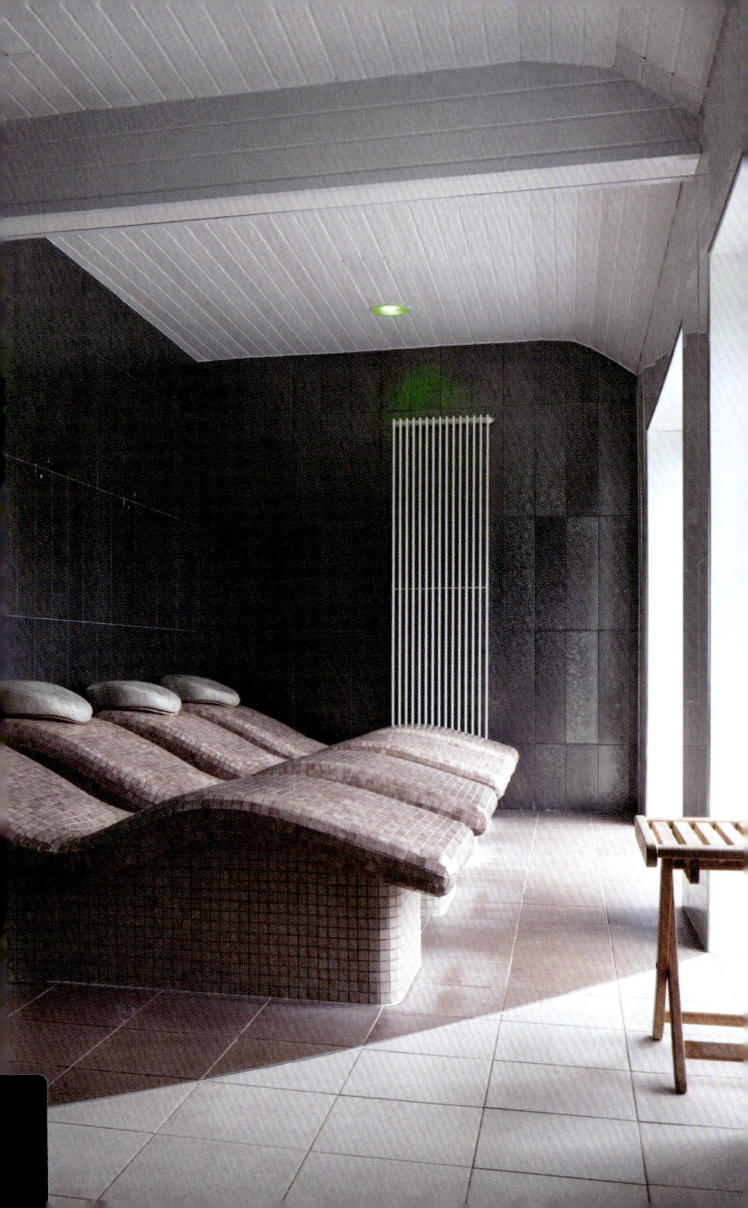

Formby Hall Golf Resort & Spa
Set in 80 hectares of reclaimed marshland 20km north of the centre, Formby Hall has two well-regarded nine- and 18-hole links golf courses plus a residential PGA academy. Since the 2008 addition of the spa, however, its feminine side has become a compelling draw. Before your visit, take a bracing stroll along this beautiful stretch of windswept coast, backed by pine trees. Then you can make truly deserved use of the 20m indoor pool, sauna, gym and ESPA treatments, as well as dry flotation, Atlas Rasul mud and steam rooms. This is a city that likes to get dolled up, of course. Local lasses also head to the spas at Knowsley Hall (T 489 4827), in the ancestral grounds of the Stanley family, and The House (T 724 4999), set in a lovely Georgian property. *Southport Old Road, T 01704 875 699, www.formbyhallgolfresort.co.uk*

Royal Birkdale Clubhouse
This 1935 art moderne clubhouse designed by architect George Tonge overlooks the 18th green of Royal Birkdale's famous golf course, sitting low in a landscape of dune and grass like a stealth craft making its way towards the Irish Sea. Its nautical appearance – flat roofs originally designed for sunbathing or tennis; polygonal and round bay windows – turns the fairways into choppy waves of green. The building was refurbished in time for the 2008 Open by Owen Ellis Architects, keeping faithful to the style (although previous extensions had not followed Tonge). This is England's self-proclaimed Golf Coast. There are also challenging courses at The West Lancashire Golf Club (T 924 1076) in Crosby and Royal Liverpool (T 632 3101) on the Wirral.
Waterloo Road, T 01704 552 020,
www.royalbirkdale.com

SPORTS

ESCAPES

WHERE TO GO IF YOU WANT TO LEAVE TOWN

It's said that Liverpudlians are more drawn to the high seas than the rest of England, so escaping this city by water follows a noble tradition. The Isle of Man catamaran glides down the Mersey before taking a sharp left at Formby and docking at Douglas three hours later. Rent a car once you're there and take on some of the infamous TT roads. Liverpool's fierce rival, Manchester, can also be reached by boat, down the Ship Canal from the Wirral.

Nearby Chester (see p101) is one of the wealthiest towns in the UK and boasts the trappings of the idle rich. Make sure you're as perfectly turned out as a footballer's wife by visiting The Club and Spa (DoubleTree by Hilton, Warrington Road, T 01244 408 840) or Spa by Kasia (Grosvenor Pulford Hotel, Wrexham Road, T 01244 572 199), before dining at chef Simon Radley's Michelin-starred restaurant (Eastgate Street, T 01244 895 618) at The Grosvenor.

The Pennines (opposite) are on Liverpool's doorstep but if you have time to venture further, the great outdoors gets even greater. Veer west at Chester to cruise the idyllic North Wales coast on your way to Dolgellau and the Ffynnon hotel (Love Lane, T 01341 421 774) in Snowdonia. Or head north to the Lake District. For the full bucolic experience, reserve the Love Shack (Cunsey, T 01539 441 242), a luxury cedar, oak and larch cabin designed by Sutherland Hussey Architects that has panoramic views of Lake Windermere. *For full addresses, see Resources.*

Singing Ringing Tree

As if the rolling scenery of the Pennines weren't spectacular enough, Lancashire County Council commissioned four pieces of public art to perch on lofty sites. Our favourite of these 'Panopticons' is Tonkin Liu's *Singing Ringing Tree*, a freeze-framed twister of galvanised steel pipes that whistles in the wind high above Burnley. The *Tree* is about an hour's drive from Liverpool, but it's far more satisfying to reach it by hiking or cycling the Trans Pennine Trail. There are three more giant installations: *Colourfields* is a collaboration between Sophie Smallhorn and Jo Rippon Architecture; *Halo* is a blue LED-lit steel lattice by John Kennedy of LandLab; and Peter Meacock's *Atom* is a bronze-coated pebble nestled in Brontë sisters moorland.
Crown Point, Burnley
www.midpenninearts.org.uk/panopticons

The Hepworth Wakefield
It's well worth the 90-minute drive over the Pennines to this gallery dedicated to modernist sculptor Barbara Hepworth. Her 6m-tall *Winged Figure* is the star, but David Chipperfield's £35m building runs it close. The 2011 jumble of 10 trapezoidal blocks is angled and scaled to complement the surrounding industrial structures, and its pigmented concrete changes hue with the light and the seasons. Hepworth was born in Wakefield in 1903 and lived there until leaving at 18 to study at Leeds School of Art, where she became friends with Henry Moore. His work, including the 1936 *Reclining Figure*, appears alongside pieces by Jacob Epstein, Patrick Heron, LS Lowry and Eva Rothschild. Stop at the Yorkshire Sculpture Park (T 01924 832 631) en route. *Gallery Walk, Wakefield, T 01924 247 360, www.hepworthwakefield.org*

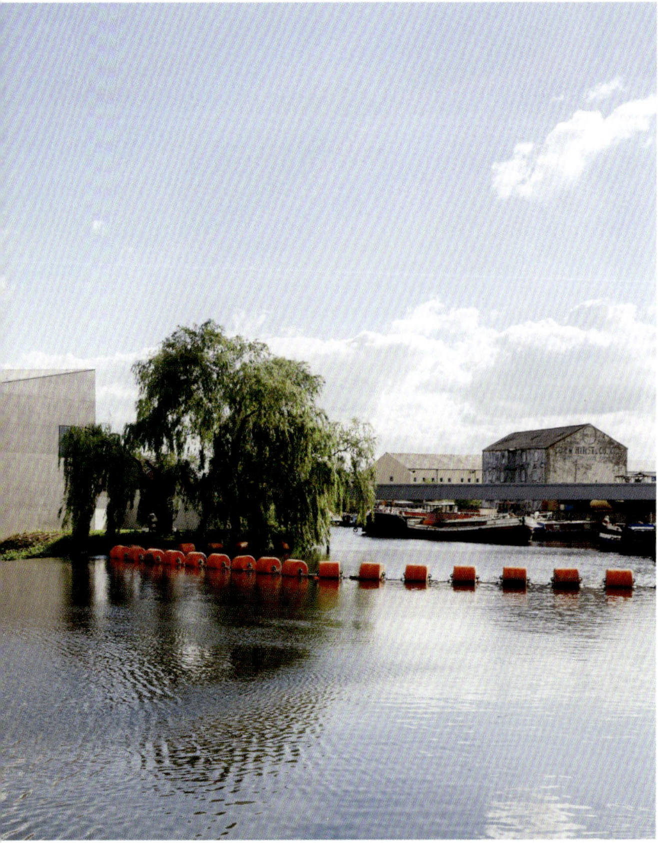

Tower of Love, Blackpool

Architects De Rijke Marsh Morgan's 2011 Tower of Love is an English seaside version of the Vegas wedding chapel. The three-storey structure is built of timber with a stainless-steel exterior that glows gold. Blackpool Tower is perfectly framed full length and phallic through a window in the ceremonial space, lending a pagan element to proceedings; downstairs is a restaurant. It is part of LDA Design's Tower Festival Headland scheme that reimagined the Blackpool seafront. It also comprises four 35m-high sculptural 'grasses' that sway in the wind and artist Gordon Young's *Comedy Carpet* (above), which covers 2,200 sq m of promenade with light-entertainment catchphrases in a variety-show poster design. Lit by Speirs + Major, it's a modern counterpoint to the town's illuminations.
Golden Mile

Oddfellows, Chester
Founded by the Romans in the 1st century AD, Chester is one of the best-preserved walled cities in Britain, boasting a plethora of medieval buildings. However, its latter-day bosses are the Cheshire Set — the millionaires, footballers, ladies-who-lunch and *Corrie* actors who have settled in this enclave just 25km from Liverpool. The old money favour The Grosvenor (T 01244 324 024), but we like to dispose of our income at Oddfellows, for its sheer chutzpah. A conversion of a 1676 mansion, the £3.3m neoclassical facade masks a riot of design. The 18 flamboyant rooms are inspired by Cestrian heroes, and in the public areas, a set table is fixed to the ceiling, *Alice in Wonderland*-style, and there's a bar in the Secret Garden's Potting Shed (above).
20 Lower Bridge Street, T 01244 895 700, www.oddfellowschester.com

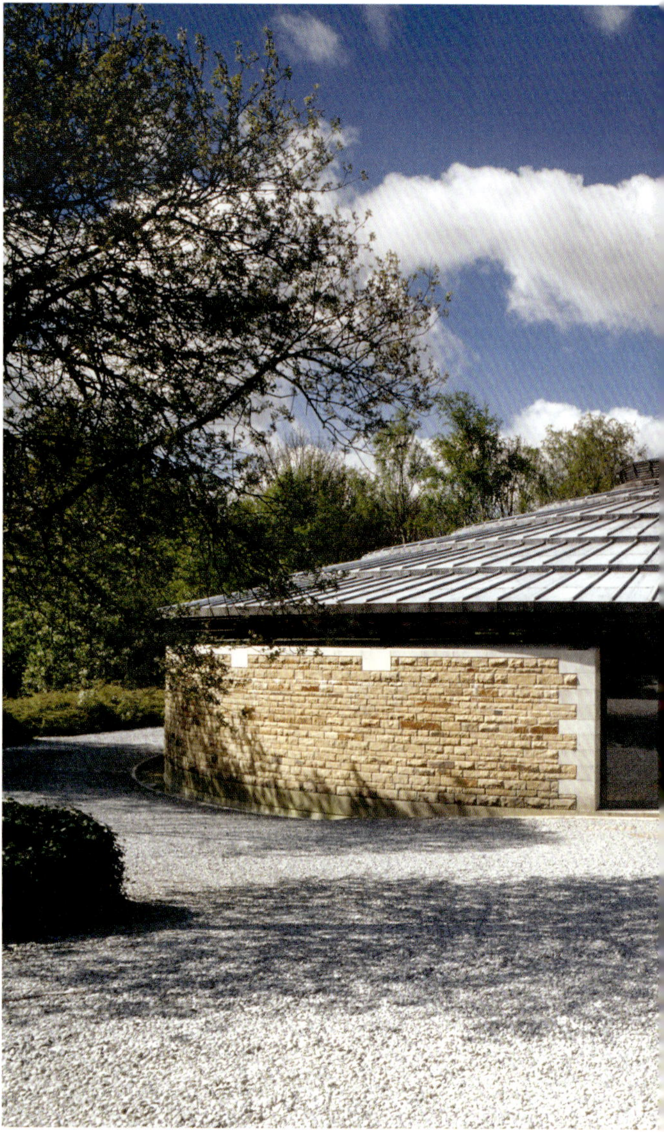

David Mellor Design Museum
Sir Michael Hopkins designed 'cutlery king' David Mellor's factory in 1990, its rustic, slab-by-slab appearance evoking the hand-finished craftsmanship taking place within; visit during the week to observe the process. The museum here tracks Mellor's work from the 1950s (he died in 2009), including his silverware and still-used 1965 traffic-light system. *Hathersage, Sheffield, T 01433 650 220*

NOTES
SKETCHES AND MEMOS

RESOURCES
CITY GUIDE DIRECTORY

A
Active Learning Lab 066
Brownlow Hill
Aintree 090
Ormskirk Road
T 523 2600
www.aintree.co.uk
Albion House 009
The Strand/James Street
Alma de Cuba 060
St Peter's Church
Seel Street
T 702 7394
www.alma-de-cuba.com
Anglican Cathedral 034
St James' Mount
T 709 6271
www.liverpoolcathedral.org.uk
Art and Design Academy 073
Brownlow Hill
T 904 1216
www.ljmu.ac.uk/lsa
Awesome Walls 089
St Albans Church
Athol Street
T 298 2422
www.awesomewalls.co.uk

B
El Bandito 051
41b Slater Street
T 707 6527
Beetham Tower 009
110 Old Hall Street
Benna 085
Rodney Street
T 0845 872 0899
www.benna.co.uk

The Bluecoat 032
School Lane
T 702 5324
www.thebluecoat.org.uk
The Bluecoat Display Centre 081
College Lane
T 709 4014
www.bluecoatdisplaycentre.com
Blueprint 080
The Bluecoat
School Lane
T 709 5297
www.thebluecoat.org.uk
Bold Street Coffee 062
89 Bold Street
T 707 0760
www.boldstreetcoffee.co.uk
Boudoir Boutique 080
14 Cavern Walks
T 231 1424
www.boudoir-boutique.com
The Brink 046
15-21 Parr Street
T 703 0582
www.thebrinkliverpool.com

C
Cabin Club 044
139 Wood Street
Cains Brewery 009
Stanhope Street
T 709 8734
www.cains.co.uk
Camp and Furnace 028
67 Greenland Street
T 708 2890
www.campandfurnace.com
The Capital 068
New Hall Place

Climbing Hangar 089
*6 Birchall Street
T 345 0587
www.theclimbinghangar.com*
The Club and Spa 096
*DoubleTree by Hilton
Warrington Road
Chester
T 01244 408 840
www.theclubandspachester.co.uk*
Corke Art Gallery 082
*296-298 Aigburth Road
T 726 0232
www.corkeartgallery.co.uk*
Cow&Co 062
*15 Cleveland Square
T 0844 858 1581
www.cowandco.co.uk*
Cricket 080
*9 Cavern Walks
T 227 4645
www.cricket-fashion.com*
Crosby Lakeside Adventure Centre 088
*Cambridge Road
Crosby
T 966 6868
www.crosbylakeside.co.uk*
Cunard Building 026
*Pier Head
www.cunardbuilding.com*

D
Da Piero 059
*5-7 Mill Hill Road
Irby
T 648 7373
www.dapiero.co.uk*

David Mellor Design Museum 102
*Hathersage
Sheffield
T 01433 650 220
www.davidmellordesign.com*
Delifonseca 062
*12 Stanley Street
T 255 0808
www.delifonseca.co.uk*

E
81LTD/Salt Dog Slims 039
*79-83 Seel Street
T 709 7172
www.saltdogslims.co.uk*
Everyman Theatre 009
*13 Hope Street
T 709 4776
www.everymanplayhouse.com*

F
FACT 030
*88 Wood Street
T 707 4464
www.fact.co.uk*
Formby Hall Golf Resort & Spa 092
*Southport Old Road
Formby
T 01704 875 699
www.formbyhallgolfresort.co.uk*
Fraiche 056
*11 Rose Mount
Oxton
T 652 2914
www.restaurantfraiche.com*

G
G-Bar 040
1-7 Erberle Street
T 236 4416
www.g-bar.com

H
Hanover Street Social 045
Casartelli Building
16-20 Hanover Street
T 709 8784
www.hanoverstreetsocial.co.uk
The Hardmans' House 027
59 Rodney Street
T 709 6261
www.nationaltrust.org.uk
The Hepworth Wakefield 098
Gallery Walk
Wakefield
West Yorkshire
T 01924 247 360
www.hepworthwakefield.org
Heroes of the Marine Engine Room 075
St Nicholas Place
Home 025
Woodside Ferry Approach
T 330 1475
62 Christchurch Road
T 653 7552
www.homecoffee.co.uk
The House 093
9 Mather Avenue
T 724 4999
www.thehousebeautyspa.co.uk
The Hub 045
16 Hanover Street
T 709 2401
www.thehub-liverpool.com

I
India Buildings 064
Water Street

K
The Kazimier 052
4-5 Wolstenholme Square
T 324 1723
www.thekazimier.co.uk
Knowsley Hall 093
Prescot
T 489 4827
www.knowsleyhallvenue.co.uk

L
Lady Lever Art Gallery 070
Lower Road
Port Sunlight
T 478 4136
www.liverpoolmuseums.org.uk
Landbaby 080
The Bluecoat
School Lane
T 07504 479 440
www.landbaby.co.uk
The Lawns 059
Thorton Hall Hotel
Neston Road
Thornton Hough
T 336 3938
www.lawnsrestaurant.co.uk
Leaf 042
65-67 Bold Street
T 707 7747
www.thisisleaf.co.uk

Littlewoods Building 010
Edge Lane
near Wavertree Botanic Gardens
Liverpool ONE Footbridge 078
Paradise Street/Hanover Street
Liverpool Watersports Centre 088
110 Mariners Wharf
T 708 9322
www.liverpoolwatersports.org.uk
The London Carriage Works 058
Hope Street
T 705 2222
www.thelondoncarriageworks.co.uk
Lunya 062
18-20 College Lane
T 706 9770
www.lunya.co.uk

M
Made Here 080
Metquarter
T 07956 852 331
www.made-here.co.uk
The Magnet 044
45 Hardman Street
T 709 4000
www.magnetliverpool.com
Martins Bank 064
4 Water Street
Maya 053
96 Wood Street
T 329 0200
Merchants Bar & Restaurant 041
56-62 Castle Street
T 702 7897
www.62castlest.com

Metropolitan Cathedral 012
Mount Pleasant
T 709 9222
www.liverpoolmetrocathedral.org.uk
MPW Steakhouse 057
Hotel Indigo
10 Chapel Street
T 559 0555
www.mpwsteakhouseliverpool.co.uk
Museum of Liverpool 014
Mann Island
T 478 4545
www.liverpoolmuseums.org.uk

N
News From Nowhere 080
96 Bold Street
T 708 7270
www.newsfromnowhere.org.uk
Nook & Willow 080
36 Seel Street
T 708 5576
www.nookandwillow.com
Nova Restaurant 059
68 Pensby Road
Heswall
T 342 9959
www.novarestaurant.co.uk

O
Open Eye Gallery 027
19 Mann Island
T 236 6768
www.openeye.org.uk

Oriel Chambers 074
14 Water Street
The Oval Lesiure Centre 088
Old Chester Road
Bebington
T 606 2010
www.wirral.gov.uk
Oxton Bar & Kitchen 056
Claughton Firs
Oxton
T 651 2535
www.oxtonbar.co.uk

P
Panoramic 34 038
34th floor
West Tower
10 Brook Street
T 236 5534
www.panoramicliverpool.com
Peninsula Dining Room 059
3 Grosvenor Road
New Brighton
T 639 8338
www.peninsula-dining-room.co.uk
Philharmonic Dining Rooms 049
36 Hope Street
T 707 2837
www.nicholsonspubs.co.uk
Philharmonic Hall 036
Hope Street
T 709 3789
www.liverpoolphil.com
Playground 016
Hilton
3 Thomas Steers Way
T 07956 374 876
www.playgroundliverpool.com

Port of Liverpool Building 026
Pier Head
Probe Records 062
School Lane
T 708 8815
www.probe-records.com
Puschka 040
16 Rodney Street
T 708 8698
www.puschka.co.uk

R
Raiders Vintage 062
38 Renshaw Street
T 709 2929
Roscoe Head 062
24 Roscoe Street
T 709 4365
www.roscoehead.co.uk
Royal Birkdale Clubhouse 094
Waterloo Road
T 01704 552 020
www.royalbirkdale.com
Royal Insurance Building 016
1-9 North John Street
Royal Liver Building 026
Pier Head
Royal Liverpool Golf Club 094
Meols Drive
T 632 3101
www.royal-liverpool-golf.com
Runcorn Bridge 013
Runcorn/Widnes

S

60 Hope Street 058
 60 Hope Street
 T 707 6060
 www.60hopestreet.com

St George's Dock Ventilation Tower 072
 The Strand
 T 227 5181
 www.merseytunnels.co.uk

St George's Hall 009
 St George's Place
 T 225 69111
 www.stgeorgesliverpool.co.uk

St Luke's Church 009
 Berry Street
 www.stlukeliverpool.co.uk

St Monica's Church 069
 Fernhill Road
 T 922 4819

Salt House Tapas 045
 1 Hanover Street
 T 706 0092
 www.salthousetapas.co.uk

Santa Chupitos 051
 41 Slater Street
 T 707 6527

Sefton Park Palm House 076
 Sefton Park
 T 726 9304
 www.palmhouse.org.uk

The Side Door 040
 29a Hope Street
 T 707 7888
 www.thesidedoor.co.uk

Simon Radley at The Grosvenor 096
 Grosvenor Hotel
 Eastgate Street
 Chester
 T 01244 895 618
 www.chestergrosvenor.co.uk

Singing Ringing Tree 097
 Crown Point
 Burnley
 www.midpenninearts.org.uk/panopticons

Spa by Kasia 096
 Grosvenor Pulford Hotel
 Wrexham Road
 Chester
 T 01244 572 199
 www.spabykasia.co.uk

Spire 040
 1 Church Road
 Wavertree
 T 734 5040
 www.spirerestaurant.co.uk

Static Gallery 082
 23 Roscoe Lane
 T 707 0770
 www.statictrading.com

Studio2 050
 33-45 Parr Street
 T 707 3727
 www.parrstreet.co.uk

Superstar Boudoir 040
 24 Stanley Street

T

Tate & Lyle Silo 009
 Regent Road
 Huskisson Dock

Tate Liverpool 064
 Albert Dock
 T 702 7400
 www.tate.org.uk

Tower of Love 100
Golden Mile
Blackpool

U
Union House 016
Victoria Street
Unity 065
3 Rumford Place
University Sports and Fitness Centre 088
Liverpool University
Peach Street
T 794 3307
www.liv.ac.uk/sports
Utility 086
60 Bold Street
T 708 4192
86 Bold Street
T 707 9919
www.utilitydesign.co.uk

V
The Vinyl Emporium 062
124 Bold Street

W
Walker Art Gallery 009
William Brown Street
T 478 4199
www.liverpoolmuseums.org.uk
The Warehouse Kitchen + Bar 054
30 West Street
Southport
T 01704 544 662
www.warehousekitchenandbar.com

Waterhouse Cafe 048
Victoria Gallery & Museum
Ashton Street
T 795 0333
www.liv.ac.uk/vgm/cafe
Weavers Door 084
1 Cavern Walks
Harrington Street
T 236 6001
www.weaversdoor.com
The West Lancashire Golf Club 094
Hall Road West
Crosby
T 924 1076
www.westlancashiregolf.co.uk
Wolstenholme Creative Space 062
11 Wolstenholme Square
www.wolstenholmecreativespace.com

Y
Yorkshire Sculpture Park 098
West Bretton
Wakefield
T 01924 832 631
www.ysp.co.uk

HOTELS
ADDRESSES AND ROOM RATES

Albany Apartments 021
Rates:
apartments, from £120
8 Old Hall Street
T 0800 699 0490 (one bedroom);
T 07778 309 671 (two bedrooms)
www.come2liverpool.com

Base2Stay 022
Room rates:
double, from £60
Secret Garden Suite, £150
29 Seel Street
T 705 2626
www.base2stay.com/liverpool

DoubleTree by Hilton 016
Room rates:
double, from £100
6 Sir Thomas Street
T 0870 590 9090
www.doubletree.com

Ffynnon 096
Room rates:
double, from £145
Love Lane
Dolgellau
Wales
T 01341 421 774
www.ffynnontownhouse.com

The Grosvenor 101
Room rates:
double, from £230
Eastgate Street
Chester
T 01244 324 024
www.chestergrosvenor.com

Hard Days Night Hotel 020
Room rates:
double, from £90;
McCartney Suite, £750;
Lennon Suite, £950
41-44 North John Street
T 236 1964
www.harddaysnighthotel.com

Heywood House Hotel 016
Room rates:
double, from £70
11 Fenwick Street
T 224 1444
www.heywoodhousehotel.co.uk

Hillbark 017
Room rates:
double, from £240
Royden Park
Frankby
T 625 2400
www.hillbarkhotel.co.uk

Hilton 016
Room rates:
double, from £110
3 Thomas Steers Way
T 708 4200
www3.hilton.com

Hope Street Hotel 018
Room rates:
double, from £70;
Room 406, £350
40 Hope Street
T 709 3000
www.hopestreethotel.co.uk

Leverhulme Hotel 017
Room rates:
double, from £150;
Room 109, £350;
Opus Grand Suite 108, £510
Port Sunlight Village
T 644 6655
www.leverhulmehotel.co.uk

Love Shack 096
Rates:
from £450 (three-night minimum stay)
Cunsey
Ambleside
Cumbria
T 01539 441 242
www.lakedistrictloveshack.com

Malmaison 016
Room rates:
double, from £175
7 William Jessop Way
T 229 5000
www.malmaison.com

Oddfellows 101
Room rates:
double, from £160
20 Lower Bridge Street
Chester
T 01244 895 700
www.oddfellowschester.com

The Racquet Club 016
Room rates:
double, from £80
5 Chapel Street
T 236 6676
www.ainscoughs.co.uk/racquet-club

Radisson Blu 016
Room rates:
double, from £75
107 Old Hall Street
T 966 1500
www.radissonblu.co.uk

Studio2 051
Room rates:
double, from £55;
Penthouse, £150
33-45 Parr Street
17 Argyle Street
T 707 1050
www.parrstreet.co.uk

Thornton Manor 016
Room rates:
double, from £135
Thornton House
Thornton Hough
T 353 1155
www.thorntonmanor.co.uk

WALLPAPER* CITY GUIDES

Executive Editor
Rachael Moloney

Editor
Jeremy Case
Author
Neil McQuillian

Art Director
Loran Stosskopf
Art Editor
Eriko Shimazaki
Designer
Mayumi Hashimoto
Map Illustrator
Russell Bell

Photography Editor
Elisa Merlo
Assistant Photography Editor
Nabil Butt

Chief Sub-Editor
Nick Mee
Sub-Editor
Kevin Grant

Editorial Assistant
Emma Harrison

Wallpaper* Group
Editor-in-Chief
Tony Chambers
Publishing Director
Gord Ray
Managing Editor
Jessica Diamond
Acting Managing Editor
Oliver Adamson

Contributors
Stuart Haynes
Anna Johnson
Terry McKenna
Joseph Sharples

Wallpaper* ® is a registered trademark of IPC Media Limited

First published 2013

All prices are correct at the time of going to press, but are subject to change.

Printed in China

PHAIDON

Phaidon Press Limited
Regent's Wharf
All Saints Street
London N1 9PA

Phaidon Press Inc
180 Varick Street
New York, NY 10014

Phaidon® is a registered trademark of Phaidon Press Limited

www.phaidon.com

A CIP Catalogue record for this book is available from the British Library.

All rights reserved.
No part of this publication may be reproduced, stored in a retrieval system or transmitted, in any form or by any means, electronic, mechanical, photocopying, recording or otherwise, without the prior permission of Phaidon Press.

© 2013 IPC Media Limited

ISBN 978 0 7148 6426 6

PHOTOGRAPHERS

Iwan Baan
Hepworth Wakefield, pp098-099

Alan C Birch
Royal Birkdale Clubhouse, pp094-095

Susan Bockelmann/ Dennis Gilbert
Littlewoods Building, pp010-011
Metropolitan Cathedral, p012
Runcorn Bridge, p013
Museum of Liverpool, pp014-015
Leverhulme Hotel, p017
Hope Street Hotel, pp018-019
Hard Days Night Hotel, p020
Albany Apartments, p021
Base2Stay, p022, p023
Pier Head, p026
Camp and Furnace, p028, p029
FACT, pp030-031
The Bluecoat, p032, p033
Anglican Cathedral, pp034-035
Philharmonic Hall, pp036-037
Panoramic 34, p038
81LTD/Salt Dog

Slims, p039
Merchants Bar & Restaurant, p041
Leaf, pp042-043
The Magnet, p044
Hanover Street Social, p045
The Brink, pp046-047
Waterhouse Cafe, p048
Philharmonic Dining Rooms, p049
Studio2, pp050-051
The Kazimier, p052
Maya, p053
The Warehouse Kitchen + Bar, pp054-055
Fraiche, p056
MPW Steakhouse, p057
60 Hope Street, p058
The Lawns, p059
Alma de Cuba, pp060-061
Jacqueline Passmore, p063
The Capital, p068
St Monica's Church, p069
Port Sunlight, pp070-071
St George's Dock Ventilation Tower, p072
Art and Design Academy, p073
Oriel Chambers, p074
Heroes of the Marine Engine Room, p075
Sefton Park Palm House, pp076-077
Liverpool ONE Footbridge, p078, p079

Static Gallery, pp082-083
Weavers Door, p084
Benna, p085
Utility, pp086-087
Awesome Walls, p089
Formby Hall Golf Resort & Spa, p092, p093

Martine Hamilton Knight
Aintree, pp090-091

Mark McNulty
Open Eye Gallery, p027

Neil McQuillian
Liverpool city view, inside front cover

Peartree Digital
Sue Binns Butter Dome, p081

Tim Soar
Unity, p065

Mike Tonkin
Singing Ringing Tree, p097

Andreas von Einsiedel
Round Building, David Mellor Design Museum, pp102-103

Hassan & Ahmed Yasin
Home, p025

LIVERPOOL
A COLOUR-CODED GUIDE TO THE HOT 'HOODS

BALTIC TRIANGLE
The city's latest regeneration hotspot retains strong links to the area's seafaring past

LIME STREET/WILLIAM BROWN STREET
Grand gestures such as the Adelphi Hotel greet you on arrival at the Victorian rail hub

CENTRAL DOCKS
Take a walk through the port's industrial past from Albert Dock to the Tobacco Warehouse

ROPEWALKS/CHINATOWN
Site of a plethora of dynamic developments, but also more than 70 listed buildings

UNIVERSITY QUARTER/GEORGIAN QUARTER
Liverpool's cultural and academic heart is also a rich architectural hunting ground

MOORFIELDS
A real mixed bag, this enclave's remit runs from Beatlemania to the business district

COMMERCIAL DISTRICT
Opened in 2008, the £1bn Liverpool ONE complex has revived the city's retail fortunes

BIRKENHEAD
It's worth taking a ferry 'cross the Mersey to visit handsome Hamilton Square alone

For a full description of each neighbourhood, see the Introduction.
Featured venues are colour-coded, according to the district in which they are located.